SERMONS
ON
JOHN 3:16

SERMONS
ON
JOHN 3:16

*"For God so loved the world, that He gave
His only begotten Son, that whosoever believeth
in Him should not perish, but have
everlasting life."*

COMPILED BY

STANLEY BARNES

AMBASSADOR

Belfast Northern Ireland **Greenville** South Carolina

SERMONS ON JOHN 3:16
© 1999 Ambassador Productions

ISBN 1   84030   066   3

Ambassador Publications
a division of
Ambassador Productions Ltd.
Providence House
16 Hillview Avenue,
Belfast, BT5 6JR
Northern Ireland

Emerald House
1 Chick Springs Road, Suite 203
Greenville,
South Carolina 29609, USA
www.emeraldhouse.com

CONTENTS

INTRODUCTION

This compilation of sermons by famous preachers of the past, provides for us a rich resource of material on one of the best loved texts of the Bible, John 3:16. Martin Luther, the great reformer, described it as the gospel in a nutshell.

Ten pulpit giants, selected from a variety of historical and doctrinal backgrounds, such as C. H. Spurgeon; Bishop Ryle; Charles Finney and Samuel Davies, offer us wonderful insights into what must be the most well known of Christ's sayings.

The inclusion of these preachers in this volume is not an endorsement of everything they have said or written, but I believe that the aim of each of these great men of God, was to preach Christ with compassion and love for those who are lost in their sin.

Only eternity itself will reveal how many souls, out of that great multitude which no man can number, have like myself, been led to Christ through the words of this favourite text of the Bible.

Stanley Barnes
September, 1999

DR. J. SIDLOW BAXTER

D r. J. Sidlow Baxter was born in Sydney, Australia, and was brought to England in his childhood. He was converted to Christ at an early age, and he trained for the ministry at Spurgeon's College, London.

After twenty-five years in the pastorate, eighteen of which were spent in Scotland, as pastor of Charlotte Chapel, Edinburgh, Dr. Baxter went into a wider ministry as a Bible teacher and conference speaker, both in Great Britain and the United States. The Doctor of Divinity degree was conferred on him by the Central Baptist Seminary, Toronto, Canada.

He became known, among evangelicals all over the English speaking world, as preacher, lecturer and author.

Among his best known books are: *Explore The Book; Awake My Heart; His Part And Ours; Mark These Men* and *The Best Word Ever* from which this sermon is taken.

1

THAT WORD 'PERISH'

'Should not perish' - John 3:16

A man once came to C. H. Spurgeon, with a poser from the Bible. 'There now,' he said, 'can you tell me what *that* means?' With a twinkle in his eye, Spurgeon replied: 'Why, of course I can tell you what it means. *It means just what it says.*' Now it is a strange fact that many of us, when we read the great invitations and solemn warnings of God's Word, vaguely assent to them without really believing that they mean *just what they say.* As it was with the man in the Gospel narrative, who cried: 'Lord, I believe; help Thou mine unbelief,' so today there is a kind of unbelieving believing; and it is very common. Many persons will tell us that they believe in Jesus; and yet they obviously do not trust or obey or love or serve Him, or in any way relate their life to Him. Many persons will tell us they believe that Jesus died on the Cross to be our Saviour; yet they have never received Jesus as their own personal Saviour, nor does it appear ever to have occurred to them that they needed to do so. Many persons will readily affirm that Jesus rose from the grave; yet they live as though He were dead. Many persons will admit belief in a coming Judgment Day; yet they live as though they were utterly unaccountable to a holy God. This unbelieving believing is strangely paradoxical, but it is common enough. It is a kind of believing merely with the upper part of the mind which leaves the heart itself undisturbed. If it were a *real* believing it would stir the heart and move the will and change the life.

How many people there are who readily believe the words of our text and yet do not believe them at all! Yet never were more tremendous words written than these - 'That whosoever believeth in Him should not *perish*, but have everlasting life.' May we ourselves not be guilty of carelessly nodding to them without thoughtfully heeding them! May God's Spirit burn into our hearts the realisation that these solemn and glorious words really mean *just what they say!*

DOES THE WORD REALLY MEAN PERISH?

Yes, these words mean just what they say; and they tell us the *purpose* which lies behind all God's loving and giving as revealed in the Gospel, namely, that we might be *eternally saved.* There is no getting over that ugly word 'perish'. It is actually in the text; and it means just what it says - 'that whosoever believeth in Him should not *perish*'. It may be asked if that word 'perish' is a true translation here. Does the Greek word so translated really mean 'perish'? The answer is that our English word 'perish' is not even a shade too harsh to represent the Greek word here. If we wish to verify this we can easily turn to other verses where this Greek word occurs. For instance, it comes in Matthew 5:29, where we have our Lord's solemn words: 'If thy right eye offend thee, pluck it out, and cast it from thee, for it is profitable for thee that one of thy members should *perish*, and not that thy whole body should be cast into hell'. It comes again in Matthew 8:25, where we find the almost shipwrecked disciples exclaiming: 'Lord, save us; we *perish*!' And again it turns up in chapter 9:17, where Jesus, speaking of the old-time skin bottles, says: 'Neither do men put new wine into old bottles, else the bottles break, and the wine runneth out, and the bottles *perish*'. Sometimes this Greek word is translated by our word 'destroy'. It is thus rendered in Matthew 2:13: 'Arise, and take the young child and his mother, and flee into Egypt, and be thou there until I bring thee word; for Herod will seek the young child to *destroy* him'. Here, then, are a few occurrences of this Greek word, chosen almost at random from the first book of the New Testament. As an example of its use elsewhere in the New Testament, take 1 Corinthians 10:9,10, where our English word 'destroyed' is again used to translate it: 'Neither let us tempt Christ, as some of them (the old-time Israelites) tempted, and were *destroyed* of serpents. Neither murmur ye, as some of them also murmured, and were *destroyed* of the destroyer'.

There can be no doubt, then, that this word in John 3:16 really means 'perish'. The plucked-out eye perishes. The sailor, if he is drowned, perishes. The burst skin-bottle perishes. The young child, if murdered, perishes. The serpent-bitten Israelites perished.

THE WORD AS USED OF THE SOUL

Yes, all these instances are quite clear but the awful thing is that in John 3:16 this word 'perish' is used in a *spiritual* sense. In all the passages just cited the word is used in a physical sense only. The plucked-out eye and the burst skin-bottle are physical things, and the perishing is a physical perishing. When the word is used of the sailor drowned in the deep, or of the infant slain by the sword, it means the death of the body, a perishing physically. The serpent-bitten Israelites who died long ago perished physically, inasmuch as their carcasses fell in the wilderness. But here, in John 3:16, the word is used of the *soul*. There is always the underlying thought of tragedy even when we speak merely about the perishing of the body; but what a depthless tragedy must the perishing of a *soul* be! When the body perishes it gradually decomposes; so that besides having lost all *consciousness*, it loses any separate *existence*: but the soul does not perish with, or like, the body: it does not lose either its

11

existence or its individual consciousness. Nothing is more plainly taught in Scripture than that. What then, can this word 'perish' mean, as used of the soul? It must mean something awful; for, as the word 'perish' is used to denote the extreme evil which can overtake the body, so, in being now used of the soul, it is obviously meant to denote the extreme evil which can befall the soul.

THE WORD IN ITS DREAD MEANING

As used of physical things, the word 'perish' always carries the thought of *destruction*. The plucked-out eye is destroyed. The burst bottle is destroyed. The drowned sailor and the infant slain by the sword are destroyed. The serpent-bitten Hebrews, whose carcasses perish in the wilderness, are destroyed. That thought of destruction is always present in the word 'perish,' when used of things physical. So is it when the word is used of the soul; though here, of course, since the soul is non-physical, it does not imply destruction in the sense of extinction, or cessation of consciousness. It signifies a final *condition* of the soul. It means the destruction of all those qualities within the soul which constitute its true life and well-being, with the consequent expulsion of the soul, in the eternal Beyond, from that environment in which alone it can know joy. Sin entered the human race through our first parents, and has prevailed within the race ever since, distancing man from God, in a spiritual sense, so that now - to quote the words of Scripture - by their hereditary nature, men are 'alienated from the life of God, through the ignorance that is in them'; and it is this state of alienation from God which makes the soul the prey of those evil dispositions which, unless expurgated by regeneration, ultimately sink it into the abysmal ruin indicated in this word 'perish'.

DAMNATION BY JUDICIAL SENTENCE

We are not just giving the rein to morbid imagination when we speak of souls being 'lost' in the hereafter. There is no mistaking the warnings of God's Word. Moreover, it is well to realise that the Scriptures attribute this final tragedy of the soul to two factors - to a judicial *sentence* passed upon the soul by the Divine Judge, and to a *process* operating within the soul itself. Plainly enough do the Scriptures pre-announce a final judgement at which sentence will be passed on souls. Equally plainly do they teach that the basis of this judgement will be 'the *deeds* done in the body', and that the sentence will be 'according to their *works*'. Twice over, in his description of the coming judgement, John says: 'They were judged … according to their *works*' (Revelation 20:12,13). This is as one would expect, for sentence is always passed on what a man has *done*, not upon what he *is*. In other words, sentence has to do with transgression, not with condition. Let us keep this clearly in mind, then, that the destiny of souls is, in one aspect, the outcome of a sentence which is passed and a penalty which is imposed. That awful reality which the Scriptures call 'the lake of fire' and 'the second death', is said to be a *penalty* for sin. It is not the only penalty; but it is the *extreme* penalty. Well may we cry in the ears of impenitent sinners: 'It is a fearful thing to fall into the hands of the living God!'

DAMNATION BY SPIRITUAL PROCESS

But there is that other aspect, equally real and awful, namely, that souls are lost through a *process* operating within the soul itself. In other words, that final tragedy of the soul, in the beyond, is the culmination of that which goes on in the soul in this present life on earth. There are those who go on in ways of sin fondly dreaming that somehow, in the end, they will elude the sentence of the dread judge. They certainly never will elude that 'great white throne' before which mankind will be arraigned; but even if they *could*, would that spare them from torment? Not at all: for their hell will be kindled by what they *are* in themselves, by the natural and inevitable culmination of their progressive sinning. We are so constituted, as human beings, that we simply cannot sin without suffering. Our condition in the *next* life is inseparable from our character in *this* life. In the fields of eternal destiny we reap as we have sown. If I read my Bible rightly, heaven and hell are real places: but the fact to grasp just here is that what makes heaven or hell in the after-sphere is not so much *where* we are as *what* we are. It has been often and truly said that 'heaven is a prepared place for a prepared people'. Heaven begins in the *heart,* down here, before it is consummated in the *home,* up there. And what is true of heaven, in this sense, is true of hell. Many a man's hell will be *himself.* The flames of Gehenna will be but the final, inescapable, quenchless burnings of those pampered passions and lusts which have been allowed to inflame the soul in this present life; so that even if a man might possibly escape sentence from his divine Judge, he simply cannot escape from *himself.*

AN INESCAPABLE CULMINATION

How awful, then, is it to live in ways of sin during this present life on earth! There is no escape, 'God is not mocked: whatsoever a man soweth, that shall he also reap'. Foolishly enough, men and women have imagined that if death did not end all for them, then at any rate they would start all over anew in the other realm. One of the greatest purposes of the New Testament is to warn us against such a foolish misconception, and to open our eyes wide to this fact that we cannot possibly escape the outworking of the process which goes on in the soul in this present life and is culminated in the eternal beyond.

Away in a tropical country, a traveller was attacked by a snake. He fled from it, but it pursued him. Almost breathless he came to a river and plunged through to the other side, so that the flowing water might mercifully separate him from his danger. But scarcely had he reached the farther bank before he heard the hiss of the reptile behind him, and on looking round saw to his horror that it had followed him through the river - it was a water snake! Even so do men's sins follow them through the river of death, and find them out in the life beyond. Moses never spoke a truer word than when he said: 'Be sure your sin will find you out'. Some men's sins find them out, and exact their sorry toll, even in this present life. Those who have lived impurely or inebriately are often 'found out' by loathsome disease of the body. Those other kinds of sinning which do not scourge us with such outward, physical retribution, find us out, none the less in our minds. No man can ever secretly indulge evil thoughts without finding that eventually his whole mind becomes a cage of unclean birds, a den of toads and reptiles, a malarial swamp, an internal hell, from which he screams to escape but without avail.

All sin finds us out in some way, because of that process which is ever going on in human souls, just as all holy aspirings and heavenward strivings bring their certain reward. We cannot extricate ourselves from this process; and even those sins which do not find us out in this present life cross the dark river with us, and sting the soul with their burning venom in the life beyond. Death may bring about a separation of soul and body, but it cannot dissolve the soul itself, or separate a man from what he is in himself. As the tree falls, so it lies; and as a man dies, so he goes into eternity. The drunkard takes his mad craving, and the glutton his inflamed appetites. The miser takes his frenzied greed, and the man enslaved to foul habits takes his deadly chains. The sensual man takes his insatiate passions, and the man of violent hate his maddening tempers. These cravings and passions will create a hell of their own, quite apart from any sentence passed by the divine Judge; for they will rage like a fever, without there being any possibility of gratification. Surely this is 'the worm that dieth not' and 'the fire that is not quenched'. If the rich man lifted up his eyes in Hades, 'being in torments' (Luke 16:23), what must it be to become engulfed in that 'lake of fire' which is Gehenna! Oh, what a woeful depth of meaning there is in that word 'perish'! We would urge every soul without Christ to pause and reflect on these words of our text - 'that whosoever believeth in Him should not *perish...*'

A PRESENT PROCESS

We have already pointed out that the word 'perish' here points to that final condition of ruin which is the *culmination* of a present process; but it is well to stress the fact that inasmuch as this process is even now operating in this present life, those souls which are closed against Christ are *even now perishing*. That this is so is clearly taught in the pages of the New Testament. Take the following verses, from the Revised Version. In 1 Corinthians 1:18, Paul says: 'The word of the Cross is foolishness *to them that are perishing*'. In 2 Corinthians 4:3, we read: 'If our Gospel is veiled, it is veiled in *them that are perishing*'. Again in 2 Thessalonians 2:10, we are told that the antichrist shall deceive *'them that are perishing'* because they have 'received not the love of the truth, that they might be saved'.

Incidentally, such verses as these are a sure *test* by which we may know whether we ourselves are among the perishing or not. Take the first of them - 'The word of the Cross is foolishness to them that are perishing'. Is the Cross of Jesus, as the one way of salvation, something which I treat with superior scorn? - then I am perishing. Those who know the power of that Cross to justify the repentant and believing sinner, glory in it. If I disdain the Cross, then that is proof enough that I am not saved by it, and that I am perishing in my unbelief. Take the next verse -'If our gospel is veiled, it is veiled in them that are perishing'. Is the warm and shining message of God's redeeming love something which leaves me coldly unmoved? Is Christ merely as 'a root out of dry ground', having 'no form nor comeliness' that I should desire Him? - then I am perishing; for Satan has cast his dark veil over my heart lest I should see the light of the Gospel and the beauty of Christ. This, indeed, is what the verse says - 'If our gospel is veiled, it is veiled in them that are perishing; in whom the god of this world hath blinded the minds of the unbelieving, that the light of the gospel of the glory of Christ, who is the image of God, should not dawn upon them'. Yes, if the Gospel is veiled to me, I am perishing.

Take the third verse, which speaks of the antichrist deceiving 'them that are perishing' because they have 'received not the love of the truth, that they might be saved'. Am I knowingly refusing to receive 'the truth as it is in Christ Jesus'? - then I am perishing; for this is the only truth that regenerates the soul. Did I once have 'the love of the truth', so that I was glad to hear the Gospel, whereas now, through prolonged procrastination to receive the Saviour, my heart has grown impervious, so that I have lost even 'the *love* of the truth'? - then I am certainly perishing.

Oh, my friends, it is an awful thing to perish! We would urge every Christless soul: Be wise to escape that eternal damnation, which is called 'the lake of fire' and 'the second death'. Make haste to the hill called Calvary. See there the only begotten Son of God making atonement for all our sin. Look to Him by faith and be saved. Open the heart to His incoming; for He who hung there long ago now knocks at the heart's door. He is no longer on the Cross, for His atonement is a completed work. He is no longer in the grave, for death is a conquered foe. None need perish, for God now offers pardon and a full salvation to all who turn from their sins and accept the Saviour. Come now to the Good Shepherd who gave His life for the sheep; for He says of all His sheep: - 'I give unto them eternal life, and they shall *never perish*'. Oh, look to Him now. Give ear to this wonderful Gospel which calls to us down the years - 'God so loved the world that He gave His only begotten Son, that whosoever believeth in Him *should not perish*, but have everlasting life'.

FRANCIS WILLIAM BOREHAM

Francis William Boreham was born in Tunbridge Wells, England. As a young man he became a clerk, but unfortunately an accident led to the loss of his foot and a permanently weakened leg. On New Year's Day in 1886 he was converted to Christ, and soon after he commenced study for the ministry at Spurgeon's College, London.

Before completing his studies, he received a call to Mosgiel, New Zealand, and he began his ministry there.

His first volume of sermons was published in 1903, but he also wrote for local papers, and he edited *The New Zealand Baptist*. He was called to Hobart and then to Melbourne, where he ministered until 1928, after which time he devoted himself to writing and itinerant preaching.

Christ was always central to his ministry, and thousands of his forty-six books were sold every year.

Among his best known writings were *My Pilgrimage* and *A Handful Of Stars* from which this sermon *'Everybody's Text'* is taken.

2

EVERYBODY'S TEXT

ONE

Centuries seemed like seconds that day: they dwindled down to nothing. It was a beautiful September morning: I was only a little boy: and, as a great treat, my father and mother had taken me to London to witness the erection of Cleopatra's Needle. The happenings of that eventful day live in my memory as vividly as though they had occurred but yesterday. I seem even now to be watching the great granite column, smothered with its maze of hieroglyphics, as it slowly ascends from the horizontal to the perpendicular, like a giant waking and standing erect after his long, long sleep. All the way up in the train we had been talking about the wonderful thing I was so soon to see. My father had told me that it once stood in front of the great temple at Heliopolis; that the Pharaohs drove past it repeatedly on their way to and from the palace; and that, very possibly, Moses, as a boy of my own age, sat on the steps at its base learning the lessons that his tutor had prescribed. It seemed to bring Moses and me very near together. To think that he, too, had stood beside this self-same obelisk and had puzzled over the weird inscriptions that looked so bewildering to me! And now Heliopolis, the City of the Sun, has vanished! A single column tells the traveller where it stood! London is the world's metropolis today. And the monument, that stood among the splendours of the *old* world is being re-erected amidst the glories of the *new!*

Will a time ever come, I wondered, when London will be as Heliopolis is? Will the Needle, in some future age, be erected in some new capital - in the metropolis of Tomorrow? Had you stood, three thousand years ago, where St. Paul's now stands, the only sound that you would have heard coming up from the forests around would have been the baying of the wolves. Wild swine ranged undisturbed along the site of the Strand. But Egypt was in her glory, and the Needle stood in front of the temple! Where, I wonder, will it stand in three thousand years' time? Some such thought must have occurred to the authorities who are presiding over its erection. For see, in the base of the obelisk a huge cavity yawns! What is to be placed within it? What greeting shall we send from the *Civilisation-that-is to the Civilisation-that-is-to-be?* It is to a strange list upon which the officials have decided. It includes a set of coins, some specimens of weights and measures, some children's toys, a London directory, a bundle of newspapers, the photographs of the twelve most beautiful women of the period, a box of hairpins and other articles of feminine adornment, a razor, a parchment containing a translation of the hieroglyphics on the obelisk itself - the hieroglyphics that so puzzled Moses and me - and last, but not least, *a text!* Yes, a text; and a text, not in one language, but in every language known! The men who tear down the obelisk from among the crumbling ruins of London may not be able to decipher this language, or that, or the other. But surely one of these ten score of tongues will have a meaning for them! And so, in the speech of these two hundred and fifteen peoples, these words are written out: FOR GOD SO LOVED THE WORLD, THAT HE GAVE HIS ONLY BEGOTTEN SON, THAT WHOSOEVER BELIEVETH IN HIM SHOULD NOT PERISH, BUT HAVE EVERLASTING LIFE. *That* is the greeting which the Twentieth Century sends to the Fiftieth! I do not know what those men - the men who rummage among the ruins of London - will make of the newspapers, the parchments, the photographs and the hairpins. I suspect that the children's toys will seem strangely familiar to them: a little girl's doll was found by the archaeologists among the ruins of Babylon: childhood keeps pretty much the same all through the ages. But the text! The text will seem to those far-off people as fresh as the latest fiftieth century sensation. Those stately cadences belong to no particular time and to no particular clime. Ages may come and go; empires may rise and fall: they will still speak with fadeless charm to the hungry hearts of men. They are for the Nations-that-were, for the Nations-that-are, and for the Nations-yet-to-be. That Text is EVERYBODY'S TEXT.

TWO

Few things are more arresting than the way in which these tremendous words have won the hearts of all kinds and conditions of men. I have been reading lately the lives of some of our most eminent evangelists and missionaries; and nothing has impressed me more than the conspicuous part that this text has played in their personal lives and public ministries. Let me reach down a few of these volumes.

Here is the *Life of Richard Weaver.* In the days immediately preceding his conversion, Richard was a drunken and dissolute coal miner. It is a rough, almost repulsive, story. He tells us how, after his revels and fights, he would go home to his mother with bruised and bleeding face. She always received him tenderly; bathed his wounds; helped him to bed; and then murmured in his ear the words that at last seemed inseparable from the sound of her voice: *'God so loved the world, that He gave His only begotten Son, that whosoever believeth in Him should not perish, but have everlasting life.'* The words came back to him in the hour of his greatest need. His soul was passing through deep waters. Filled with misery and shame, and terrified lest he should have sinned beyond the possibility of salvation, he crept into a disused sandpit. He was engaged to fight another man that day, but he was in death-grips with a more terrible adversary. 'In that old sand-pit,' he says, 'I had a battle with the devil; and I came off more than conqueror through Him that loved me.' And it was the text that did it. As he agonised there in the sand-pit, tormented by a thousand doubts, his mother's text all at once spoke out bravely. It left no room for uncertainty. *'God so loved the world, that He gave His only begotten Son, that whosoever believeth in Him should not perish, but have everlasting life.'* 'I thought,' Richard tells us, 'that *whosoever* meant *me*. What faith was, I could not tell; but I had heard that it was taking God at His word; and so I took God at His word and trusted in the finished work of my Saviour. The happiness I then enjoyed I cannot describe; my peace flowed as a river.'

Duncan Matheson and Richard Weaver were contemporaries. They were born at about the same time; and, at about the same time they were converted. Matheson was Scottish; Weaver was English. Matheson was a stonemason; Weaver was a coal-miner; in due course both became evangelists. In some respects they were as unlike each other as two men could possibly be: in other respects their lives are like sister ships; they seem exactly alike. Especially do they resemble each other in their earliest religious experiences. We have heard Weaver's story: let us turn to Matheson's. Weaver, at the time of his conversion, was twenty-five: Matheson is twenty-two. He has been ill at ease for some time, and every sermon he has heard has only deepened his distress. On a sharp winter's morning, with the frost sparkling on the shrubs and plants around him, he is standing in his father's garden, when, suddenly, the words of Richard Weaver's text - Everybody's Text - take powerful hold upon his mind. 'I saw,' he says, 'that God loves me, for God loves all the world. I saw the proof of His love in the giving of His Son. I saw that *whosoever* meant *me, even me*. My load was loosed from off my back. Bunyan describes his pilgrim as giving three leaps for joy as his burden rolled into the open sepulchre. I could not contain myself for gladness.' The parallel is very striking.

'God loves me!' exclaims Richard Weaver, in surprise.

'I saw that God loves me!' says Duncan Matheson.

'I thought that "whosoever" meant "me",' says Weaver.

'I saw that "whosoever" meant "me",' says Matheson.

'The happiness I then enjoyed I cannot describe,' says our English coal-miner.

'I could not contain myself for gladness,' says our Scottish stonemason.

We may dismiss the evangelists with that, and turn to the missionaries.

THREE

Like Richard Weaver and Duncan Matheson, Frederick Arnot and Egerton R. Young were contemporaries. I heard them both - Fred Arnot in Exeter Hall and Egerton Young in New Zealand. They lived and laboured on opposite sides of the Atlantic. Fred Arnot gave himself to the fierce Barotses of Central Africa; Egerton Young set himself to win the Red Men of the North American woods and prairies.

Arnot's life is one of the most pathetic romances that even Africa has given to the world. He made the wildest men love him. Sir Francis de Winton declares that Arnot made the name of Englishman fragrant amidst the vilest habitations of cruelty. 'He lived a life of great hardship,' says Sir Ralph Williams; 'I have seen many missionaries under varied circumstances, but such an absolutely forlorn man, existing on from day to day, almost homeless, without any of the appliances that make life bearable, I have never seen.' And the secret of this great unselfish life? The secret was the text. He was only six when he heard Livingstone. He at once vowed that he, too, would go to Africa. When his friends asked how he would get there, he replied that, if that were all, he would swim. But nobody knew better than he did that the real obstacles that stood between himself and a life like Livingstone's were not physical but spiritual. He could not lead Africa into the kingdom of Christ unless he had first entered that kingdom himself. As a boy of ten, he found himself lying awake at two o'clock one morning, repeating a text. He went over it again and again and again. *'God so loved the world, that He gave His only begotten Son, that whosoever believeth in Him should not perish, but have everlasting life.'* 'This,' says Sir William Robertson Nicoll, 'was Arnot's lifelong creed, and he worked in its spirit.' 'This,' he says himself, 'was my first and chief message.' He could imagine none greater.

Exactly so was it with Egerton Young. He tells us, for example, of the way in which he invaded the Nelson River district and opened work among people who had never before heard the gospel. He is surrounded by two hundred and fifty or three hundred wild Indians. 'I read aloud,' he says, 'those sublime words: *"For God so loved the world, that He gave His only begotten Son, that whosoever believeth in Him should not perish, but have everlasting life."* They listened with the most rapt attention whilst for four hours I talked to them of the truths of this glorious verse. When I had finished, every eye turned towards the principal chief. He rose, and, coming near me, delivered one of the most thrilling addresses I have ever heard. Years have passed away since that hour, and yet the memory of that tall, straight, impassioned Indian is as vivid as ever. His actions were many, but all were graceful. His voice was particularly fine and full of pathos, for he spoke from the heart.'

"Missionary," exclaimed the stately old chief, "I have not, for a long time, believed in our religion. I hear God in the thunder, in the tempest and in the storm: I see His power in the lightning that shivers the tree: I see His goodness in giving us the moose, the reindeer, the beaver, and the bear. I see His loving-kindness in sending us, when the south winds blow, the ducks and geese; and when the snow and ice melt away, and our lakes and rivers are open again, I see how He fills them with fish. I have watched all this for years, and I have felt that the Great Spirit, so kind and watchful and loving, could not be pleased by the beating of the conjurer's drum or the shaking of the rattle of the medicine man. And so I have had no religion. But what you have just said fills my heart and satisfies its longings. I am so glad you have come with this wonderful story. Stay as long as you can!"

Other chiefs followed in similar strains; and each such statement was welcomed by the assembled Indians with vigorous applause.

The message of the text was the very word that they had all been waiting for.

Fred Arnot found that it was what *AFRICA* was waiting for!

Egerton Young found that it was what *AMERICA* was waiting for!

It is the word that *ALL THE WORLD* is waiting for! For that text is *Everybody's Text!*

FOUR

A pair of evangelists - Weaver and Matheson!

A pair of missionaries - Arnot and Young!

I have one other pair of witnesses waiting to testify that this text is *Everybody's Text*. Martin Luther and Lord Cairns have very little in common. One was German; the other was English. One was born in the fifteenth century; the other in the nineteenth. One was a monk; the other was Lord Chancellor. But they had *this* in common, that they had to die. And when they came to die, they turned their faces in the same direction. Lord Cairns, with his parting breath, quietly but clearly repeated the words of *Everybody's Text*. *"God so loved the world, that He gave His only begotten Son, that whosoever believeth in Him should not perish, but have everlasting life."*

During his last illness, Luther was troubled with severe headaches. Someone recommended to him an expensive medicine. Luther smiled.

'No,' he said, 'my best prescription for head and heart is that *God so loved the world, that He gave His only begotten Son, that whosoever believeth in Him should not perish, but have everlasting life.'*

A fortnight before he passed away, he repeated the text with evident ecstasy, and added 'What Spartan saying can be compared with this wonderful brevity? It is a Bible in itself!' And in his dying moments he again repeated the words, thrice over, in Latin.

'They are the best prescription for headache and heartache!' said Luther.

There were headaches and heartaches in the world three thousand years ago, when Cleopatra's Needle stood beside the Temple at Heliopolis!

There will be headaches and heartaches in the world centuries hence, when the obelisk is rescued from among the ruins of London!

There were headaches and heartaches among those Barotse tribes to whom Fred Arnot went!

There were headaches and heartaches among those tattooed braves to whom Egerton Young carried the message.

There are headaches and heartaches in England, as the Lord Chancellor knew!

There are headaches and heartaches in Germany, as Luther found!

And, because there are headaches and heartaches for everybody, this is *Everybody's Text*. There is, as Luther said, nothing like it.

FIVE

When Sir Harry Lauder was here in Melbourne, he had just sustained the loss of his only son. His boy had fallen at the front. And, with this in mind, Sir Harry told a beautiful and touching story. 'A man came to my dressing-room in a New York theatre,' he said, 'and told of an experience that had recently befallen him. In American towns, any household that had given a son to the war was entitled to place a star on the window-pane. Well, a few nights before he came to see me, this man was walking down a certain avenue in New York accompanied by his wee boy. The lad became very interested in the lighted windows of the houses, and clapped his hands when he saw the star . As they passed house after house, he would say, "Oh, look, Daddy, there's another house that has given a son to the war! And there's another! There's one with two stars! And look, there's a house with no star at all!" At last they came to a break in the houses. Through the gap could be seen the evening star shining brightly in the sky.

The little fellow caught his breath. "Oh, look, Daddy," he cried, "God must have given *His* Son, for He has got a star in *His* window."

'He has, indeed!' said Harry Lauder, in repeating the story.

But it took the clear eyes of a little child to discover that the very stars are repeating *Everybody's Text*. The heavens themselves are telling of the love that gave a Saviour to die for the sins of the world.

SAMUEL DAVIES

S amuel Davies was born in Delaware of Welsh parents, on 3rd November, 1723. Although the exact date of his conversion is not known, he did make a public confession of his faith in Christ when he was fifteen years of age. He received his theological training from Samuel Blair at Foggs Manor in Pennsylvania and was licensed to preach in that state in 1746, Shortly afterwards, however, with his new bride Sarah Kirkpatrick, he moved to Virginia, where he served as an evangelist and organiser of dissenting congregations. He gained the reputation of encouraging the Great Southern Awakening during colonial times.

Along with Gilbert Tennent, founder of the Log College, he came to the United Kingdom in 1753 to raise money for the College of New Jersey, later to be known as Princeton University, and found many who were ardent supporters of the Great Awakening. Following the death in 1758 of Jonathan Edwards, the President of the College, Davies was chosen as his successor, but he himself died of pneumonia in 1761, just eighteen months after taking up the position.

Although he will be remembered for his leadership at the College of New Jersey, he was, however, first and foremost, a preacher of God's Word.

This sermon, on John 3:16 was preached in October 1757, shortly after his recovery from a severe illness.

3

THE METHOD OF SALVATION THROUGH JESUS CHRIST

For God so loved the world, that He gave His only begotten Son, that whosoever believeth in Him should not perish, but have everlasting life. John 3:16

I have been solicitously thinking in what way my life, redeemed from the grave, may be of most service to my dear people. And I would collect all the feeble remains of my strength into one vigorous effort this day, to promote this benevolent end. If I knew what subject has the most direct tendency to save your souls, that is the subject to which my heart would cling with peculiar endearment, and which I would make the matter of the present discourse.

And when I consider I am speaking to an assembly of sinners, guilty, depraved, helpless creatures, and that, if ever you be saved, it will only be through Jesus Christ, in the way which the gospel reveals; when I consider that your everlasting life and happiness turn upon this hinge, namely, the reception you give to this Saviour, and this way of salvation; I say, when I consider these things, I can think of no subject I can more properly choose than to recommend the Lord Jesus to your acceptance, and to explain and inculcate the method of salvation through his mediation; or, in other words, to preach the pure gospel to you; for the gospel, in the most proper sense, is nothing else but a revelation of a way of salvation for sinners of Adam's race.

My text furnishes me with proper materials for my purpose. Let heaven and earth hear it with wonder, joy, and raptures of praise! *'God so loved the world, that He gave His only begotten Son, that whosoever* (or that everyone that) *believeth in Him should not perish, but have everlasting life.'*

This is a part of the most important evening conversation that ever was held; I mean, that between Christ and Nicodemus, a Pharisee and ruler of the Jews. Our Lord first instructs him in the doctrine of regeneration, that grand constituent of a Christian, and pre-requisite to our admission in the kingdom of heaven; and then He proceeds to inform him of the gospel method of salvation, which contains these two grand articles, the death of Christ, as the great foundation of blessedness; and faith in Him, as the great qualification upon the part of the sinner. He presents this important doctrine to us in various forms, with a very significant repetition. *'As Moses lifted up the serpent in the wilderness, even so must the Son of Man be lifted up'*; (that is, hung on a cross,) *'that whosoever believeth in Him should not perish, but have everlasting life.'* Then follows my text, which expresses the same doctrine with great force: *'God so loved the world, that He gave His only begotten Son, gave Him up to death, that whosoever believeth in Him should not perish, but have everlasting life.'* He goes on to mention a wonder. This earth is a rebellious province of Jehovah's dominions, and therefore if His Son should ever visit it, one would think it would be as an angry judge, or as the executioner of His Father's vengeance. But, O astonishing! *'God sent not His Son into the world to condemn the world, but that the world through Him might be saved.'* Hence the terms of life and death are thus fixed. *'He that believeth on Him is not condemned: but he that believeth not is condemned already, because he hath not believed in the name of the only begotten Son of God.'* Sure the heavenly rivers of pleasure flow in these verses. Never, methinks, was there so much gospel expressed in so few words. Here, take the gospel in miniature, and bind it to your hearts for ever. These verses alone, methinks, are a sufficient remedy for a dying world.

The truths I would infer from the text for present improvement are these:

1. That without Christ you are all in a perishing condition;
2. That through Jesus Christ a way is opened for your salvation;
3. That the grand pre-requisite to your being saved in this way, is faith in Jesus Christ;
4. That every one, without exception, whatever his former character has been, that is enabled to comply with this pre-requisite, shall certainly be saved;
   and
5. That the constitution of this method of salvation, or the mission of Christ into our world, as the Saviour of sinners, is a most striking and astonishing instance and display of the love of God.

1. MY TEXT IMPLIES, THAT WITHOUT CHRIST YOU ARE ALL IN A PERISHING CONDITION

This holds true of you in particular, because it holds true of the world universally; for the world was undoubtedly in a perishing condition without Christ, and none but He could relieve it, otherwise God would never have given His only begotten Son to save it. God is not ostentatious or prodigal of His gifts, especially of so inestimable a gift as His Son, whom He loves infinitely more than the whole creation. So great, so dear a person would not have been sent upon a mission which could have been discharged by any other being. Thousands of rams must bleed in sacrifice, or ten thousands of rivers of oil must flow; our first-born must die for our transgressions, and the fruit of our body for the sin of our souls; or Gabriel, or some of the upper ranks of angels, must leave their thrones, and hang upon a cross, if such methods of salvation had been sufficient. All this would have been nothing in comparison of the only begotten Son of God leaving His native heaven, and all its glories, assuming our degraded nature, spending thirty-three long and tedious years in poverty, disgrace, and persecution, dying as a malefactor and a slave in the midst of ignominy and torture, and lying a mangled breathless corpse in the grave. We may be sure there was the highest degree of necessity for it, otherwise God would not have given up His dear Son to such a horrid scene of sufferings.

This, then, was the true state of the world, and consequently yours without Christ; it was hopeless and desperate in every view. In that situation there would not have been so much goodness in the world as to try the efficacy of sacrifices, prayers, tears, reformation, and repentance, or they would have been tried in vain. It would have been inconsistent with the honour of the divine perfections and government, to admit sacrifices, prayers, tears, repentance, and reformation, as a sufficient atonement.

What a melancholy view of the world have we now before us! We know the state of mankind only under the gracious government of a Mediator; and we but seldom realise what our miserable condition would have been, had this gracious administration never been set up. But exclude a Saviour in your thoughts for a moment, and then take a view of the world - helpless! hopeless! - under the righteous displeasure of God; and despairing of relief! - the very suburbs of hell! the range of malignant devils! the region of guilt, misery and despair! - the mouth of the infernal pit! - the gate of hell! - This would have been the condition of our world had it not been for that Jesus who redeemed it; and yet in this very world He is neglected and despised.

But you will ask me, 'How it comes that the world was in such an undone, helpless, hopeless condition without Christ; or what are the reasons of all this?'

The true account of this will appear from these two considerations, that all mankind are sinners; and that no other method but the mediation of Christ could render the salvation of sinners consistent with the honour of the divine perfections and government, with the public good, and even with the nature of things.

All mankind are sinners. This is too evident to need proof. They are sinners, rebels against the greatest and best of beings, against their Maker, their liberal Benefactor, and their rightful Sovereign, to whom they are under stronger and more endearing obligations than they can be under to any creature, or even to the entire system of creatures; sinners, rebels in every part of our guilty globe; none righteous, no, not one; all sinners, without exception: sinners from age to age for thousands of years: thousands, millions, innumerable multitudes of sinners. What an obnoxious race is this! There appears no difficulty in the way of justice to punish such creatures. But what seeming insuperable difficulties appear in the way of their salvation! Let me mention a few of them to recommend that blessed Saviour who has removed them all.

If such sinners be saved, how shall the holiness and justice of God be displayed? How shall he give an honourable view of himself to all worlds as a being of perfect purity, and an enemy to all moral evil?

If such sinners be saved, how shall the honour of the divine government and law be secured? How will the dignity of the law appear, if a race of rebels may trifle with it with impunity? What a sorry law must that be that has no sanctions, or whose sanctions may be dispensed with at pleasure? What a contemptible government, that may be insulted and rejected, and the offender admitted into favour without exemplary punishment? No government can subsist upon such principles of excessive indulgence.

How can such sinners be saved, and yet the good of the public secured, which is always the end of every wise and good ruler? By the public good I do not mean the happiness of mankind alone, but I mean the happiness of all worlds of reasonable creatures collectively, in comparison of which the happiness of mankind alone may be only a private interest, which should always give way to the public good. Now sin has a direct tendency, not only according to law, but according to the nature of things, to scatter misery and ruin wherever its infection reaches. Therefore the public good cannot properly be consulted without giving a loud and effectual warning against all sin, and dealing with offenders in such a manner as to deter others from offending. But how can this be done? How can the sinner be saved, and yet the evil of sin displayed, and all other beings be deterred from it for ever? How can sin be discouraged by pardoning it? its evil displayed by letting the criminal escape punishment? These are such difficulties, that nothing but divine wisdom could ever surmount them.

These difficulties lie in the way of a mere pardon, and exemption from punishment: but salvation includes more than this. When sinners are saved, they are not only pardoned, but received into high favour, made the children, the friends, the courtiers of the King of heaven. They are not only delivered from punishment, but also advanced to a state of perfect positive happiness, and nothing short of this can render such creatures as we happy. Now, in this view, the difficulties rise still higher, and it is the more worthy of observation, as this is not generally the case in human governments; and as men are apt to form their notions of the divine government by human, they are less sensible of these difficulties. But this is indeed the true state of the case here; how can the sinner be not only delivered from punishment but also advanced to a state of perfect happiness? not only escape the displeasure of his offended Sovereign, but be received into full favour, and advanced to the highest honour and dignity; how can this be done without casting a cloud over the purity and justice of the Lord of all; without sinking his law and government into contempt; without diminishing the evil of sin, and emboldening others to venture upon it, and so at once injuring the character of the supreme Ruler, and the public good? How can sinners, I say, be saved without the salvation being attended with these bad consequences?

And here you must remember, that these consequences must be provided against. To save men at random, without considering the consequences, to distribute happiness to private persons with an undistinguishing hand, this would be at once inconsistent with the character of the supreme Magistrate of the universe, and with the public good. Private persons are at liberty to forgive private offences; nay, it is their duty to forgive; and they can hardly offend by way of excess in the generous virtues of mercy and compassion. But the case is otherwise with a magistrate; he is obliged to consult the dignity of his government and the interest of the public; and he may easily carry his lenity to a very dangerous extreme, and by his tenderness to criminals do an extensive injury to the state. This is particularly the case with regard to the great God, the universal supreme Magistrate of all worlds. And this ought to be seriously considered by those men of loose principles among us, who look upon God only under the fond character of a father, or a being of infinite mercy; and thence conclude, they have little to fear from him for all their audacious iniquities. There is no absolute necessity that sinners should be saved: justice may be suffered to take place upon them. But there is the most absolute necessity that the Ruler of the world should both be, and appear to be holy and just. There is the most absolute necessity that he should support the dignity of his government, and guard it from contempt, that he should strike all worlds with a proper horror of sin, and represent it in its genuine infernal colours, and so consult the good of the whole, rather than a part. There is, I say, the highest and most absolute necessity for these things; and they cannot be dispensed with as matters of arbitrary pleasure. And unless these ends can be answered in the salvation of men, they cannot be saved at all. No, they must all perish, rather than God should act out of character, as the supreme Magistrate of the universe, or bestow private favours to criminals, to the detriment of the public.

And in this lay the difficulty. Call a council of all the sages and wise men of the world, and they can never get over this difficulty, without borrowing assistance from the gospel. Nay, this, no doubt, puzzled all the angelic intelligences, who pry so deep into the mysteries of heaven, before the gospel was fully revealed.- Methinks the angels, when they saw the fall of man, gave him up as desperate. 'Alas! (they cried) the poor creature is gone! he and all his numerous race are lost for ever.' This, they knew, had been the doom of their fellow-angels that sinned: and could they hope better for man? Then they had not seen any of the wonders of pardoning love and mercy, and could they have once thought that the glorious person, who filled the middle throne, and was their Creator and Lord, would ever become a man, and die, like a criminal, to redeem an inferior rank of creatures? No, this thought they would probably have shuddered at as blasphemy.

And must we then give up ourselves and all our race as lost beyond recovery? These are huge and seemingly insuperable difficulties in the way; and we have seen that neither men nor angels can prescribe any relief. But, sing, O ye heavens, for the Lord hath done it, shout, ye lower parts of the earth: break forth into singing, ye mountains, O forest, and every tree therein; for the Lord hath redeemed Jacob, and glorified himself in Israel, Isaiah 44:23. Which leads me to add,

2. MY TEXT IMPLIES, THAT THROUGH JESUS CHRIST A WAY IS OPENED FOR YOUR SALVATION

He, and he only was found equal to the undertaking; and before him all these mountains became a plain; all these difficulties vanish; and now God can be just, can secure the dignity of his character, as the Ruler of the world, and answer all the ends of government, and yet justify and save the sinner that believeth in Jesus.

This is plainly implied in this glorious epitome of the gospel: God so loved the world, that He gave His only begotten Son, that whosoever believeth in Him should not perish, but have everlasting life. Without this gift all was lost: but now, whosoever believeth in Him may be saved; saved in a most honourable way. This will appear more particularly, if we consider the tendency the mediation of Christ had to remove the difficulties mentioned. But I would premise two general remarks.

The first is, That God being considered in this affair in his public character, as Supreme Magistrate, or Governor of the world, all the punishment which he is concerned to see inflicted upon sin is only such as answers the ends of government. Private revenge must vent itself on the very person of the offender, or be disappointed. But to a ruler, as such, it may in some cases be indifferent, whether the punishment be sustained by the very person that offended, or by a substitute suffering in his stead. It may also be indifferent whether the very same punishment, as to kind and degree, threatened in the law, be inflicted, or a punishment equivalent to it. If the honour of the ruler and his government be maintained, if all disobedience be properly discountenanced; if, in short, all the ends of government can be answered, such things as these are indifferences. Consequently, if these ends should be answered by Christ's suffering in the stead of sinners, there would be no objection against it. This remark introduces another, namely, (2.) That Jesus Christ was such a person that His suffering as the substitute or surety of sinners, answered all the ends of government which could be answered by the execution of the punishment upon the sinners themselves. To impose suffering upon the innocent, when unwilling, is unjust; but Jesus was willing to undertake the dreadful task. And besides, He was a person (sui juris) at His own disposal, His own property, and therefore He had a right to dispose of His life as He pleased; and there was a merit in His consenting to that which He was not obliged to previous to His consent. He was also a person of infinite dignity, and infinitely beloved by His Father; and these considerations rendered the merit of His sufferings for a short time, and another kind of punishment than that of hell, equal, more than equal to the everlasting sufferings of sinners themselves. Jesus Christ was also above law; that is, not obliged to be subject to that law which he had made for His creatures, and consequently His obedience to the law, not being necessary for himself, might be imputed to others: whereas creatures are incapable of works of supererogation, or of doing more than they are bound to do, being obliged to obey their divine law-giver for themselves to the utmost extent of their abilities, and consequently their obedience, however perfect, can be sufficient only for themselves, but cannot be imputed to others. Thus it appears, in general, that the ends of government are as effectually answered by the sufferings of Christ in the room of sinners, as they could be by the everlasting punishment of the sinners themselves; nay, we shall presently find they are answered in a more striking and illustrious manner. To mention particulars:

Was it necessary that the holiness and justice of God should be displayed in the salvation of sinners? See how bright they shine in a suffering Saviour! Now it appears that such is the holiness and justice of God, that He will not let even His own Son escape unpunished, when He stands in the law-place of sinners, though guilty only by the slight stain (may I so speak) of imputation. Could the execution of everlasting punishment upon the hateful criminals themselves ever give so bright a display of these attributes? It were impossible. Again,

Was it a difficulty to save sinners, and yet maintain the rights of the divine government, and the honour of the law? See how this difficulty is removed by the obedience and death of Christ! Now it appears, that the rights of the divine government are so sacred and inviolable, that they must be maintained, though the darling Son of God should fall a sacrifice to justice; and that not one offence against this government can be pardoned, without his making a full atonement. Now it appears, that the Supreme Ruler is not to be trifled with, but that His injured honour must be repaired, though at the expense of His Son's blood and life. Now, the precept of the law is perfectly obeyed in every part, and a full equivalent to its penalty endured, by a person of infinite dignity; and it is only upon this footing, that is, of complete satisfaction to all the demands of the law, that any of the rebellious sons of men can be restored into favour. This is a satisfaction which Christ alone could give: to sinners it is utterly impossible, either by doing or suffering. They cannot do all the things that are written in the law; nor can they endure its penalty, without being for ever miserable: and therefore the law has received a more complete satisfaction in Christ that it would ever receive from the offenders themselves. Further,

Was it a difficulty how sinners might be saved, and yet the evil of sin be displayed in all its horrors? Go to the cross of Christ; there, ye fools, that make a mock of sin, there learn its malignity, and its hatefulness to the great God. There you may see it is so great an evil, that when it is but imputed to the man, that is God's fellow, as the surety of sinners, it cannot escape punishment. No, when that dreadful stain lay upon Him, immediately the commission was given to divine justice, *'Awake, O sword, against my Shepherd, and against the man that is my fellow, saith the Lord of hosts; smite the Shepherd.'* Zechariah 13:7. - When Christ stood in the room of sinners, even the Father spared not His own Son, but gave Him up to death. That the criminals themselves, who are an inferior race of creatures, should not escape would not be strange: but what an enormous evil must that be, which cannot be connived at even in the favourite of heaven, the only begotten Son of God! Surely nothing besides could give so striking a display of its malignity!

Was it a difficulty how to reconcile the salvation of sinners, and the public good? that is, how to forgive sins, and yet give an effectual warning against it? How to receive the sinner into favour, and advance him to the highest honour and happiness, and in the mean time deter all other beings from offending? All this is provided for in the sufferings of Christ as a surety. Let all worlds look to His cross, and receive the warning which His wounds, and groans, and blood, and dying agonies proclaim aloud; and sure they can never dare to offend after the example of man. Now they may see that the only instance of pardon to be found in the universe was brought about by such means as are not likely to be repeated; by the incarnation and death of the Lord of glory. And can they flatter themselves that He will leave His throne and hang upon a cross, as often as any of his creatures wantonly dare to offend Him? No; such a miracle as this, the utmost effort of divine grace, is not often to be renewed; and therefore, if they dare to sin, it is at their peril. They have no reason to flatter themselves they shall be favoured like fallen man; but rather to expect they shall share in the doom of the fallen angels.

Or if they should think sin may escape with but a slight punishment, here they may be convinced of the contrary. If the Darling of heaven, the Lord of glory, though personally innocent, suffers so much when sin is but imputed to Him, what shall the sinners themselves feel, who can claim no favour upon the footing of their own importance, or personal innocence? If these things be done 'in the green tree, what shall be done in the dry?'

Thus, my brethren, you may see how a way is opened through Jesus Christ for our salvation. All the ends of government may be answered, and yet you pardoned, and made happy. Those attributes of the divine nature, such as mercy and justice, which seemed to clash, are now reconciled; now they mingle their beams, and both shine with a brighter glory in the salvation of sinners, than either of them could apart. And must you not acknowledge this divine God-like scheme? Can you look round you over the works of the creation, and see the divine wisdom in every object, and can you not perceive the divine agency in this still more glorious work of redemption? Redemption, which gives a full view of the Deity, not as the sun in eclipse, half dark, half bright, but as

A God all o'er consummate, absolute,
Full orb'd, in his whole round of rays complete. -Young.

39

And shall not men and angels join in wonder and praise at the survey of this amazing scheme? Angels are wrapt in wonder and praise, and will be so to all eternity. See! how they pry into this mystery! hark! how they sing! 'Glory to God in the highest;' and celebrate the Lamb that was slain! and shall not men, who are personally interested in the affair, join with them? Oh! are there none to join with them in this assembly? Surely, none can refuse!

Now, since all obstructions are removed on God's part, that lay in the way of our salvation, why should we not all be saved together? What is there to hinder our crowding into heaven promiscuously? Or what is there requisite on our part, in order to make us partakers of this salvation? Here it is proper to pass on to the next truth inferred from the text, namely:

3. **THAT THE GRAND PRE-REQUISITE TO YOUR BEING SAVED IN THIS WAY, IS FAITH IN JESUS CHRIST.**

Though the obstructions on God's part are removed by the death of Christ, yet there is one remaining in the sinner, which cannot be removed without his consent; and which, while it remains, renders his salvation impossible in the nature of things; that is, the depravity and corruption of his nature. Till this is cured, he cannot relish those fruitions and employments in which the happiness of heaven consists, and consequently he cannot be happy there. Therefore there is a necessity, in the very nature of things, that he should be made holy, in order to be saved; nay, his salvation itself consists in holiness. Now, faith is the root of all holiness in a sinner. Without a firm realising belief of the great truths of the gospel, it is impossible a sinner should be sanctified by their influence: and without a particular faith in Jesus Christ he cannot derive from Him those sanctifying influences by which alone he can be made holy, and which are conveyed through Jesus Christ, and through Him alone.

Further: It would be highly incongruous, and indeed impossible, to save a sinner against his will, or in a way he dislikes. Now faith, as you shall see presently, principally consists in a hearty consent to and approbation of the way of salvation through Jesus Christ, the only way in which a sinner can be saved consistently with the divine honour: so that the constitution of the gospel is not only just, but as merciful as it can be, when it ordains that only, *'he that believeth shall be saved; but that he that believeth not, shall be damned.'*

Again: We cannot be saved through Jesus Christ, till His righteousness be so far made ours as that it will answer the demands of the laws for us, and procure the favour of God to us; but His righteousness cannot be thus imputed to us, or accounted ours in law, till we are so united to Him as to be one in law, or one legal person with Him. Now faith is the bond of union; faith is that which interests us in Christ; and therefore without faith we cannot receive any benefit from His righteousness.

Here then a most interesting inquiry presents itself: 'What is it to believe in Jesus Christ? or what is that faith which is the grand pre-requisite to salvation?' If you are capable of attention to the most interesting affair in all the world, attend to this with the utmost seriousness and solemnity.

Faith in Christ includes something speculative in it; that is, it includes a speculative rational belief, upon the testimony of God, that Jesus Christ is the only Saviour of men. But yet it is not entirely a speculation, like the faith of multitudes among us: it is a more practical, experimental thing; and that you may understand its nature, you must take notice of the following particulars.

i. Faith pre-supposes a deep sense of our undone, helpless condition. I told you before, this is the condition of the world without Christ; and you must be sensible at heart that this is your condition in particular, before you can believe in Him as your Saviour. He came to be a Saviour in a desperate case, when no relief could possibly be had from any other quarter, and you cannot receive Him under that character till you feel yourselves in such a case; therefore, in order to your believing, all your pleas and excuses for your sins must be silenced, all your high conceit of your own goodness must be mortified, all your dependence upon your own righteousness, upon the merit of your prayers,

41

your repentance, and good works, must be cast down, and you must feel that indeed you lie at mercy, that God may justly reject you for ever, and that all you can do can bring Him under no obligation to save you. These things you must be deeply sensible of, otherwise you can never receive the Lord Jesus Christ in that view in which He is proposed to you, namely, as a Saviour in a desperate case.

I wish and pray you may this day see yourselves in this true, though mortifying light. It is the want of this sense of things that keeps such crowds of persons unbelievers among us. It is the want of this that causes the Lord Jesus to be so little esteemed, so little sought for, so little desired among us. In short, it is the want of this that is the great occasion of so many perishing from under the gospel, and, as it were, from between the hands of a Saviour. It is this, alas! that causes them to perish, like the impenitent thief on the cross, with a Saviour by their side. O that you once rightly knew yourselves, you would then soon know Jesus Christ, and receive salvation from his hand.

ii. Faith implies the enlightening of the understanding to discover the suitableness of Jesus Christ as a Saviour, and the excellency of the way of salvation through Him. While the sinner lies undone and helpless in himself, and looking about in vain for some relief, it pleases a gracious God to shine into his heart, and enables him to see His glory in the face of Jesus Christ. Now this once neglected Saviour appears not only absolutely necessary, but also all-glorious and lovely, and the sinner's heart is wrapt away, and for ever captivated with His beauty: now the neglected gospel appears in a new light, as different from all his former apprehensions as if it were quite another thing. I have not time at present to enlarge upon this discovery of Christ and the gospel which faith includes; and indeed should I dwell upon it ever so long, I could not convey just ideas of it to such of you as have never had the happy experience of it. In short, the Lord Jesus, and the way of salvation through

Him, appear perfectly suitable, all-sufficient, and all-glorious: and in consequence of this,

iii. The sinner is enabled to embrace this Saviour with all his heart, and to give a voluntary, cheerful consent to this glorious scheme of salvation. Now all his former unwillingness and reluctance are subdued, and his heart no more draws back from the terms of the gospel, but he complies with them, and that not merely out of constraint and necessity, but out of free choice, and with the greatest pleasure and delight. How does his heart now cling to the blessed Jesus with the most affectionate endearment! How is he lost in wonder, joy, and gratitude, at the survey of the divine perfections, as displayed in this method of redemption! How does he rejoice in it, as not only bringing happiness to him, but glory to God; as making his salvation not only consistent with, but a bright illustration of, the divine perfections, and the dignity of his government! While he had no other but the low and selfish principles of corrupt nature, he had no concern about the honour of God; if he might be but saved, it was all he was solicitous about: but now he has a noble, generous heart; now he is concerned that God should be honoured in his salvation, and this method of salvation is recommended and endeared to him by the thought that it secures to God the supremacy, and makes his salvation subservient to the divine glory.

iv. Faith in Jesus Christ implies an humble trust or dependence upon him alone for the pardon of sin, acceptance with God, and every blessing. As I told you before, the sinner's self-confidence is mortified; he gives up all hope of acceptance upon the footing of his own righteousness; he is filled with self-despair, and yet he does not despair absolutely; he does not give up himself as lost, but has cheerful hopes of becoming a child of God, and being for ever happy, guilty and unworthy as he is; and what are these hopes founded upon? Why, upon the mere free grace and mercy of God, through the righteousness of Jesus Christ. On this he ventures a guilty, unworthy, helpless soul, and finds it a firm, immovable foundation, while every other ground of dependence proves but a quicksand. There are many that flatter themselves they put their trust in God; but their trust wants sundry qualifications essential to a true faith. It is not the trust of a humble helpless soul that draws all its encouragement from the mere mercy of God, and the free indefinite offer of the gospel; but it is the presumptuous trust of a proud self-confident sinner, who draws his encouragement in part at least from his imaginary goodness and importance. It is not a trust in the mercy of God through Jesus Christ, as the only medium through which it can be honourably conveyed; but either in the absolute mercy of God, without a proper reference to a Mediator, or in his mercy, as in some measure deserved or moved by something in the sinner. Examine whether your trust in God will stand this test.

I have now given you a brief answer to that grand question, What is it to believe in Jesus Christ? and I hope you understand it, though I have not enlarged so much upon it as I willingly would. I shall only add, that this faith may also be known by its inseparable effects; which are such as follow. Faith purifies the heart, and is a lively principle of inward holiness. Faith is always productive of good works, and leads to universal obedience: faith overcomes the world and all its temptations: faith realises eternal things, and brings them near; and hence it is defined by the apostle, *'The substance of things hoped for, the evidence of things not seen.'* Hebrews 11:1. Here I have a very important question to propose to you: Who among you can say, 'Well, notwithstanding all my imperfections, and all my doubts and fears, I cannot but humbly hope, after the best examination I can make, that such a faith has been produced in this heart of mine?' And can you say so indeed? Then I bring you glad tidings of great joy; you shall be saved: yes, saved you shall be, in spite of earth and hell; saved, however great your past sins have been. Which thought introduces the glorious truth that comes next in order, namely:-

4. MY TEXT IMPLIES, THAT EVERY ONE, WITHOUT EXCEPTION, WHATEVER HIS FORMER CHARACTER HAS BEEN, THAT IS ENABLED TO BELIEVE IN JESUS CHRIST, SHALL CERTAINLY BE SAVED

The number or aggravations of sins do not alter the case; and the reason is, the sinner is not received into favour, in whole or in part, upon the account of any thing personal, but solely and entirely upon the account of the righteousness of Jesus Christ. Now, this righteousness is perfectly equal to all the demands of the law; and therefore, when this righteousness is made over to the sinner as his by imputation, the law has no more demands upon him for great sins than for small, for many than for few; because all demands are fully satisfied by the obedience of Jesus Christ to the law. You see that sinners of all characters who believe in Him are put upon an equality in this respect: they are all admitted upon one common footing, the righteousness of Christ; and that is as sufficient for one as another.

This encouraging truth has the most abundant support from the Holy Scriptures. Observe the agreeable indefinite *whosoever* so often repeated. 'Whosoever believeth in Him, shall not perish, but have everlasting life'. Whosoever he be, however vile, however guilty, however unworthy, if he does but believe, he shall not perish, but have everlasting life. What an agreeable assurance is this from the lips of Him who has the final states of men at His disposal! The same blessed lips have also declared, *'Him that cometh unto Me, I will in no wise cast out.'* John 6:37. And *'Whosoever will, let him take the water of life freely.'* Revelation 22:17. He has given you more than bare words to establish you in the belief of this truth; upon this principle He has acted, choosing some of the most abandoned sinners to make them examples, not of His justice, as we might expect, but of His mercy, for the encouragement of others. In the days of His flesh He was reproached by His enemies for His friendship to publicans and sinners; but sure it is, instead of reproaching, we must love Him on this account. When He rose from the dead, He did not rise with angry resentment against His murderers; no, but He singles them out from a world of sinners, to make them the first offers of pardon through the blood which they had just shed. He orders *'that repentance and remission of sins should be preached in His name among all nations, beginning at Jerusalem.'* Luke 24:47. At Jerusalem, where He had been crucified a few days before, there He orders the first publication of pardon and life to be made. You may see what monsters of sin He chose to make the monuments of His grace in Corinth. *'Neither fornicators, nor idolaters, nor adulterers, nor effeminate, nor abusers of themselves with mankind. Nor thieves, nor covetous, nor drunkards, nor revilers, nor extortioners, shall inherit the kingdom of God.'* What a dismal catalogue is this! It is no wonder such a crew should not inherit the kingdom of heaven; they are fit only for the infernal prison; and yet astonishing! it follows, *'such were some of you: but ye are washed, but ye are sanctified, but ye are justified, in the name of the Lord Jesus, and by the Spirit of our God.'* 1 Corinthians 6:9-11. What sinner after this can despair of mercy upon his believing in Jesus! Paul was another instance of the same kind: 'This,' says he, 'is a faithful saying,' a saying that may be depended on as true, 'and worthy of all acceptation,' from a guilty world, *that Christ Jesus came into the world to save sinners; of whom I am chief. Howbeit, for this cause I obtained mercy, 'that in me first Jesus Christ might show forth all long suffering, for a pattern to them which should hereafter believe on Him to life everlasting.'* 1 Timothy 1:15,16. A sinner of less size would not have answered this end so well; but if Saul the persecutor obtains mercy upon his believing, who can despair?

You see upon the whole, my brethren, you are not excluded from Christ and life by the greatness of your sins; but if you perish it must be from another cause: it must be on account of your wilful unbelief in not accepting of Jesus Christ as your Saviour. If you reject Him, then indeed you must perish, however small your sins have been; for it is only His death that can make atonement for the slightest guilt; and if you have no interest in that, the guilt of the smallest sin will sink you into ruin.

Here is a door wide enough for you all, if you will but enter in by faith. Come, then, enter in, you that have hitherto claimed a horrid precedence in sin, that have been ringleaders in vice, come now take the lead, and show others the way to Jesus Christ; harlots, publicans, thieves, and murderers, if such be among you, there is salvation even for you, if you will but believe. Oh! how astonishing is the love of God discovered in this way: a consideration which introduces the last inference from my text, namely,

5. THAT THE CONSTITUTION OF THIS METHOD OF SALVATION, OR THE MISSION OF A SAVIOUR INTO OUR WORLD, IS A MOST STRIKING AND ASTONISHING DISPLAY OF THE LOVE OF GOD

'God so loved the world as to give His only begotten Son.' View the scheme all through, and you will discover love, infinite love, in every part of it Consider the great God as self-happy and independent upon all His creatures, and what but love, self-moved love, could excite Him to make such provision for an inferior part of them! Consider the world sunk in sin, not only without merit, but most deserving of everlasting punishment, and what but love could move Him to have mercy upon such a world? Consider the Saviour provided, not an angel, not the highest creature, but His Son, His only begotten Son; and what but love could move Him to appoint such a Saviour? Consider the manner in which He was sent, as a gift, a free unmerited gift; 'God gave His only begotten Son'. And what but infinite love could give such an unspeakable gift? Consider the blessings conferred through this Saviour, deliverance from perdition and the enjoyment of everlasting life, and what but the love of God could confer such blessings? Consider the condition upon which these blessings are offered, faith, the humble, self-emptied grace, so suitable to the circumstances of a poor sinner, that brings nothing, but receives all, and what but divine love could make such a gracious appointment? 'It is of faith that it might be by grace.' Romans 4:16. Consider the indefinite extent or the universality of the offer, which takes in sinners of the vilest character, and excepts

47

against none: *'Whosoever believeth shall not perish.'* Oh what love
is this! But I must leave it as the theme of your meditations, not only
in the house of your pilgrimage, but through all eternity: eternity
will be short enough to pry into this mystery, and it will employ the
understandings of men and angels through the revolutions of eternal
ages.

And now, my brethren, to draw towards a conclusion, I would
hold a treaty with you this day about the reconciliation to God through
Jesus Christ. I have this day set life and death before you: I have
opened to you the method of salvation through Jesus Christ: the
only method in which you can be saved; the only method that could
afford a gleam of hope to such a sinner as I in my late approach to
the eternal world (this sermon was preached a little after recovery
from a severe fit of sickness, and is dated Hanover, October 2, 1757).
And now I would bring the matter home, and propose it to you all to
consent to be saved in this method, or, in other words, to believe in
the only begotten Son of God; this proposal I seriously make to you:
and let heaven and earth, and your own consciences, witness that it
is made to you: I also insist for a determinate answer this day; the
matter will not admit of a delay, and the duty is so plain, that there is
no need of time to deliberate. A Roman ambassador, treating about
peace with the ambassador of a neighbouring state, if I remember
rightly, and finding him desirous to gain time by shuffling and tedious
negotiations, drew a circle about him, and said, 'I demand an answer
before you go out of this circle.' Such a circle let the walls of this
house, or the extent of my voice, be to you: before you leave this
house, or go out of hearing, I insist on a full, decisive answer of this
proposal, Whether you will believe in Jesus Christ this day, or not?

But before I proceed any farther, I would remove one stumbling-
block out of your way. You are apt to object, 'You teach us that faith
is the gift of God, and that we cannot believe of ourselves; why then
do you exhort us to it? Or how can we be concerned to endeavour
that which is impossible for us to do?'

In answer to this I grant the premises are true; and God forbid
I should so much as intimate that faith is the spontaneous growth of
corrupt nature, or that you can come to Christ without the Father's
drawing you: but the conclusions you draw from these premises are

very erroneous. I exhort and persuade you to believe in Jesus Christ, because it is while such means are used with sinners, and by the use of them, that it pleases God to enable them to comply, or to work faith in them. I would therefore use those means which God is pleased to bless for this end. I exhort you to believe in order to set you upon the trial; for it is putting it to trial, and that only, which can fully convince you of your own inability to believe; and till you are convinced of this, you can never expect strength from God. I exhort you to believe, because, sinful and enfeebled as you are, you are capable of using various preparatives to faith. You may attend upon prayer, hearing, and all the outward means of grace with natural seriousness; you may endeavour to get acquainted with your own helpless condition, and, as it were, put yourselves in the way of divine mercy; and though all these means cannot of themselves produce faith in you, yet it is only in the use of these means you are to expect divine grace to work it in you: never was it yet produced in one soul, while lying supine, lazy, and inactive.

I hope you now see good reasons why I should exhort you to believe, and also perceive my design in it; I therefore renew the proposal to you, that you should this day, as guilty, unworthy, self-despairing sinners, accept of the only begotten Son of God as your Saviour, and fall in with the gospel-method of salvation; and I once more demand your answer. I would by no means, if possible, leave the pulpit this day till I have effectually recommended the blessed Jesus, my Lord and Master, to your acceptance. I am strongly bound by the vows and resolutions of a sick bed to recommend Him to you; and now I would endeavour to perform my vows. I would have us all this day, before we part, consent to God's covenant, that we may go away justified to our houses.

To this I persuade and exhort you, in the name and by the authority of the great God, by the death of Jesus Christ for sinners, by your own most urgent and absolute necessity, by the immense blessings proposed in the gospel, and by the heavy curse denounced against unbelievers.

All the blessings of the gospel, pardon of sin, sanctifying grace, eternal life, and whatever you can want, shall become yours this day, if you but believe in the Son of God; then let desolation overrun our land, let public and private calamities crowd upon you, and make you so many Jobs for poverty and affliction, still your main interest is secure; the storms and waves of trouble can only bear you to heaven, and hasten your passage to the harbour of eternal rest. Let devils accuse you before God, let conscience indict you and bring you in guilty, let the fiery law make its demands upon you, you have a righteousness in Jesus Christ that is sufficient to answer all demands, and having received it by faith, you may plead it as your own in law. Happy souls! Rejoice in hope of the glory of God, for your hope will never make you ashamed!

But I expect, as usual, some of you will refuse to comply with this proposal. This, alas! has been the usual fate of the blessed gospel in all ages and in all countries; as some have received it, so some have rejected it. That old complaint of Isaiah has been justly repeated thousands of times; *'Who hath believed our report? and to whom is the arm of the Lord revealed?'* Isaiah 53.1. And is there no reason to pour it out from a broken heart over some of you, my dear people? Are you all this day determined to believe? If so, I pronounce you blessed in the name of the Lord; but if not, I must denounce your doom.

Be it known to you then from the living God, that if you thus continue in unbelief, you shut the door of mercy against yourselves, and exclude yourselves from eternal life. Whatever splendid appearances of virtue, whatever amiable qualities, whatever seeming good works you have, the express sentence of the gospel lies in full force against you, *'He that believeth not shall be damned.'* Mark 16:16. *'He that believeth not is condemned already, because he hath not believed in the name of the only begotten Son of God.'* John 3:18. *'He that believeth not the Son shall not see life; but the wrath of God abideth on him.'* John 3:36. This is your doom repeatedly pronounced by Him whom you must own to be the best friend of human nature; and if He condemn, who can justify you?

Be it also known to you, that you will not only perish, but you will perish with peculiar aggravations; you will fall with no common ruin; you will envy the lot of heathens who perished without the law; for oh! you incur the peculiarly enormous guilt of rejecting the gospel, and putting contempt upon the Son of God. This is a horrid exploit of wickedness, and this God resents above all the other crimes of which human nature is capable. Hence Christ is come for judgement as well as for mercy into this world, and He is set for the fall as well as the rising again of many in Israel. You now enjoy the light of the gospel, which has conducted many through this dark world to eternal day; but remember also, *this is the condemnation*; that is, it is the occasion of the most aggravated condemnation, *that light is come into the world, and men love darkness rather than light*. On this principle Jesus pronounced the doom of Chorazin and Bethsaida more intolerable than that of Sodom and Gomorrah. Matthew 11:21,22. And it would not be hard to find a place in Virginia where the doom of unbelievers is likely to be so terrible as among us?

And now does not all this move you? Are you not alarmed at the thought of perishing; of perishing by the hand of a Saviour rejected and despised; perishing under the stain of His profaned blood; perishing not only under the curse of the law, but under that of the gospel, which is vastly heavier? Oh! are you hardy enough to venture upon such a doom? This doom is unavoidable if you refuse to comply with the proposal now made to you.

I must now conclude the treaty; but for my own acquittance, I must take witness that I have endeavoured to discharge my commission, whatever reception you give it. I call heaven and earth, and your own consciences to witness, that life and salvation, through Jesus Christ, have been offered to you on this day; and if you reject it, remember it; remember it whenever you see this place; remember it whenever you see my face, or one another; remember it, that you may witness for me at the supreme tribunal, that I am clear of your blood. Alas! you will remember it among a thousand painful reflections millions of ages hence, when the remembrance of it will rend your hearts like a vulture. Many sermons forgotten upon earth are remembered in hell, and haunt the guilty mind forever. Oh that you would believe, and so prevent this dreadful effect from the present sermon!

CHARLES GRADISON FINNEY

C harles Grandison Finney was born on the 29th August, 1792 in Warren, Connecticut. It was while studying to be a lawyer, that he first began to take a serious interest in the Scriptures, and he was converted to Christ when he was twenty-nine years of age. He then studied for the Presbyterian ministry and in 1824 he was ordained in the Oneida Presbytery. For the next eight years he led revival meetings in upper New York state and in many major cities from Wilmington to Boston. During those years he established modern forms and methods of revivalism and was considered by many to be the forerunner of present day evangelism.

He then became the minister of Chatham Street Chapel in New York City, where he was renowned for his lawyer like theological lectures, and among his best known publications are his *Lectures on Revival of Religion* (1835) and *Letters on Revival* (1845).

He was also professor at Oberlin College in Ohio, becoming second president from 1851 until 1866, and serving there until his death in 1875.

The following sermon was taken from his book *Sermons on Gospel Themes*.

4

GOD'S LOVE FOR A SINNING WORLD

For God so loved the world that He gave His only begotten Son, that whosoever believeth in Him should not perish, but have everlasting life. John 3:16.

Sin is the most expensive thing in the universe. Nothing else can cost so much. Pardoned or unpardoned, its cost is infinitely great. Pardoned, the cost falls chiefly on the great atoning Substitute; unpardoned, it must fall on the head of the guilty sinner.

The existence of sin is a fact everywhere experienced - everywhere observed. There *is* sin in our race everywhere, and in awful aggravation.

Sin is the violation of an infinitely important law - a law designed and adapted to secure the highest good of the universe. Obedience to this law is naturally essential to the good of creatures. Without obedience there could be no blessedness even in heaven.

As sin is a violation of a most important law, it cannot be treated lightly. No government can afford to treat disobedience as a trifle, inasmuch as everything - the entire welfare of the government and of all the governed - turns upon obedience. Just in proportion to the value of the interests at stake is the necessity of guarding law and of punishing disobedience.

The law of God must not be dishonoured by anything *He* shall do. It has been dishonoured by the disobedience of man; hence, the more need that God should stand by it, to retrieve its honour. The utmost dishonour is done to law by disowning, disobeying, and despising it. All this, sinning man has done. Hence, this law being not only good, but intrinsically necessary to the happiness of the governed, it becomes of all things most necessary that the lawgiver should vindicate his law. He must by all means do it.

Hence, sin has involved God's government in a vast expense. Either the law must be executed at the expense of the well-being of the whole race, or God must submit to suffer the worst results of disrespect to His law - results which in some form must involve a vast expense.

Take for example any human government. Suppose the righteous and necessary laws which it imposes are disowned and dishonoured. In such a case the violated law must be honoured by the execution of its penalty, or something else not less expensive, and probably much more so, must be endured. Transgression must cost happiness, somewhere, and in vast amount.

In the case of God's government it has been deemed advisable to provide a substitute - one that should answer the purpose of saving the sinner, and yet of honouring the law. This being determined on, the next great question was - *How shall the expense be met?*

The Bible informs us how the question was in fact decided. By a voluntary conscription - shall I call it - or donation? Call it as we may, it was a voluntary offering. Who shall head the subscription? Who shall begin where so much is to be raised? Who will make the first sacrifice? Who will take the first step in a project so vast? The Bible informs us. It began with the Infinite Father. He made the first great donation. He gave His only begotten Son - this to begin with - and having given Him first, He freely gives all else that the exigencies of the case can require. First, He gave His Son to make the atonement due to law then gave and sent His Holy Spirit to take charge of this work. The Son on His part consented to stand as the representative of sinners, that He might honour the law, by suffering in their stead. He poured out His blood, made a whole life of suffering a free donation on the altar - withheld not His face from spitting, nor His back from stripes - shrunk not from the utmost contumely that wicked men could heap on Him. So the Holy Ghost also devotes Himself to most self-denying efforts unceasingly, to accomplish the great object.

It would have been a very short method to have turned over His hand upon the wicked of our race, and sent them all down quick to hell, as once He did when certain angels 'kept not their first estate.' Rebellion broke out in heaven. Not long did God bear it, around His lofty throne. But in the case of man He changed His course - did not send them all to hell, but devised a vast scheme of measures, involving most amazing self-denials and self-sacrifices, to gain men's souls back to obedience and heaven.

For whom was this great donation made? 'God so loved the World,' meaning the whole race of men. By the 'world' in this connection cannot be meant any particular part only, but the whole race. Not only the Bible, but the nature of the case shows that the atonement must have been made for the whole world. For plainly if it had not been made for the entire race, no man of the race could ever know that it was made for himself, and therefore not a man could believe on Christ in the sense of receiving by faith the blessings of the atonement. There being an utter uncertainty as to the persons embraced in the limited provisions which we now *suppose* to be made, the entire donation must fail through the impossibility of rational faith for its reception. Suppose a will is made by a rich man bequeathing certain property to certain unknown persons, described only by the name of 'the elect.' They are not described otherwise than by this term, and all agree that although the maker of the will had the individuals definitely in his mind, yet that he left no description of them, which either the persons themselves, the courts, nor any living mortal can understand. Now such a will is of necessity altogether null and void. No living man can claim under such a will, and none the better though these elect were described as residents of Oberlin. Since it does not embrace all the residents of Oberlin, and does not define which of them, all is lost. All having an equal claim and none any definite claim, none can inherit. If the atonement were made in this way, no living man would have any valid reason for believing himself one of the elect, prior to his reception of the Gospel. Hence he would have no authority to believe and receive its blessings by faith. In fact, the atonement must be wholly void - on this supposition - unless a special revelation is made to the persons for whom it is intended.

As the case is, however, the very fact that a man belongs to the race of Adam - the fact that he is human, born of woman, is all-sufficient. It brings him within the pale. He is one of the *world* for whom God gave His Son, that whosoever would believe in Him might not perish, but have everlasting life.

The subjective motive in the mind of God for this great gift was *love*, love to the world. God so loved the world that He gave His Son to die for it. God loved the universe also, but this gift of His Son sprang from love to our world. True in this great act He took pains to provide for the interests of the universe. He was careful to do nothing that could in the least let down the sacredness of His law. Most carefully did He intend to guard against misapprehension as to His regard for His law and for the high interests of obedience and happiness in His moral universe. He meant once for all to preclude the danger lest any moral agent should be tempted to undervalue the moral law.

Yet farther, it was not only from love to souls, but from respect to the spirit of the law of His own eternal reason, that He gave up His Son to die. In this the purpose to give up His Son originated. The law of His own reason must be honoured and held sacred. He may do nothing inconsistent with its spirit. He must do everything possible to prevent the commission of sin and to secure the confidence and love of His subjects. So sacred did He hold these great objects that He would baptise His Son in His own blood, sooner than peril the good of the universe. Beyond a question it was love and regard for the highest good of the universe that led Him to sacrifice His own beloved Son.

Let us next consider attentively the *nature* of this love. The text lays special stress on this -God *so* loved - His love was of such a nature, so wonderful and so peculiar in its character, that it led Him to give up His only Son to die. More is evidently implied in this expression than simply its greatness. It is most peculiar in its character. Unless we understand this, we shall be in danger of falling into the strange mistake of the Universalists, who are forever talking about God's love for sinners, but whose notions of the nature of this love never lead to repentance or to holiness. They seem to think of this love as simply good nature, and conceive of God only as a very good-natured being, when nobody need to fear. Such notions have not the least influence towards holiness, but the very opposite. It is only when we come to understand what this love is in its nature that we feel its moral power promoting holiness.

It may be reasonably asked, If God so loved the world with a love characterised by greatness, and by greatness only, why did He not save all the world without sacrificing His Son? This question suffices to show us that there is deep meaning in this word *so*, and should put us upon a careful study of this meaning.

1. This love in its nature is not *complacency* - a delight in the character of the race. This could not be, for there was nothing amiable in their character. For God to have loved such a race *complacenctly* would have been infinitely disgraceful to Himself.

2. It was not a mere emotion or feeling. It was not a blind impulse, though many seem to suppose it was. It seems to be often supposed that God acted as men do when they are borne away by strong emotion. But there could be no virtue in this. A man might give away all he is worth under such a blind impulse of feeling, and be none the more virtuous. But in saying this we do not exclude all emotion from the love of benevolence, nor from God's love for a lost world. He had emotion, but not emotion *only*. Indeed the Bible everywhere teaches us that God's love

for man, lost in his sins, was paternal - the love of a father for his offspring - in this case, for a rebellious, froward, prodigal offspring. In this love there must of course blend the deepest compassion.

3. On the part of Christ, considered as Mediator, this love was *fraternal*. 'He is not ashamed to call them *brethren*'. In one point of view He is acting for brethren, and in another for children. The Father gave Him up for this work and of course sympathises in the love appropriate to its relations.

4. This love must be altogether *disinterested*, for He had nothing to hope or to fear - no profit to make out of His children if they should be saved. Indeed, it is impossible to conceive of God as being selfish, since His love embraces all creatures and all interests according to their real value. No doubt He took delight in saving our race - why should He not? It is a great salvation in every sense, and greatly does it swell the bliss of heaven - greatly will it affect the glory and the blessedness of the Infinite God. He will eternally respect Himself for love so disinterested. He knows also that all His holy creatures will eternally respect Him for this work and for the love that gave it birth. But let it also be said, He knew they would not respect Him for this great work unless they should see that He did it for the good of sinners.

5. This love was *zealous* - not that cold-hearted state of mind which some suppose - not an abstraction, but a love, deep, zealous, earnest, burning in His soul that nothing can quench.

6. The sacrifice was a most self-denying one. Did it cost the *father* nothing to give up His own beloved Son to suffer, and to die such a death? If this be not self-denial, what can be? Thus to give up His Son to so much suffering - it not this the noblest

self-denial? The universe never could have the idea of great self-denial but for such an exemplification.

7. This love was particular because it was universal; and also universal because it was particular. God loved each sinner in particular, and therefore loved all. Because He loved all impartially with no respect of persons, therefore He loved each in particular.

8. This was a most *patient* love. How rare to find a parent so loving his child as never to be impatient. Let me go round and ask, how many of you, parents, can say that you love all your children so well, and with so much love, and with love so wisely controlling, that you have never felt impatient towards any of them - so that you can take them in your arms under the greatest provocations and love them *down*, love them out of their sins, love them into repentance and into a filial spirit? Of which your children can you say, Thank God, I never fretted against that child - of which, if you were to meet him in heaven, could you say, I never caused that child to fret? Often have I heard parents say, I love my children, but oh, how my patience fails me! And, after the dear ones are dead, you may hear their bitter moans, Oh, my soul, how could I have caused my child so much stumbling and so much sin!

But God never frets - is never impatient. His love is so deep and so great that He is always patient.

Sometimes, when parents have unfortunate children - poor objects of compassion - they can bear with anything from them; but when they are very wicked, they seem to feel that they are quite excusable for being impatient. In God's case, these are not unfortunate children, but are intensely wicked --intelligently wicked. But oh, His amazing patience - so set upon their good, so desirous of their highest welfare, that however they abuse Him, He sets himself to bless them still, and weep them down, and melt them into *penitence* and love, by the death of His Son in their stead!

9. This is a *jealous love*, not in a bad sense, but in a good sense - in the sense of being exceedingly careful lest anything should occur to injure those He loves. Just as husband and wife who truly love each other are jealous with ever wakeful jealousy over each other's welfare, seeking always to do all they can to promote each other's true interests.

This donation is already made - made in good faith - not only *promised*, but actually *made*. The promise, given long before, has been fulfilled. The Son has come, has died, has made the ransom and lives to offer it - a prepared salvation to all who will embrace it.

The Son of God died not to appease vengeance, as some seem to understand it, but under the demands of law. The law had been dishonoured by its violation. Hence, Christ undertook to honour it by giving up to its demands His suffering life and atoning death. It was not to appease a vindictive spirit in God, but to secure the highest good of the universe in a dispensation of mercy.

Since this atonement has been made, all men in the race have a right to it. It is open to every one who will embrace it. Though Jesus still remains the Father's Son, yet by gracious right He belongs in an important sense to the race - to everyone; so that every sinner has an interest in His blood if he will only come humbly forward and claim it. God sent His Son to be the Saviour of the world - of whomsoever would believe and accept this great salvation.

God gives His Spirit to apply this salvation to men. He comes to each man's door and knocks, to gain admittance, if He can, and show each sinner that he may now have salvation. Oh, what a labour of love is this!

This salvation must be received, if at all, *by faith*. This is the only possible way. God's government over sinners is moral, not physical, because the sinner is himself a moral and not a physical agent. Therefore, God can influence us in no way unless we will give Him our confidence. He never can save us by merely taking us away to some place called heaven - as if change of place would change the voluntary heart. There can, therefore, be no possible way to be saved but by simple faith.

Now do not mistake and suppose that embracing the Gospel is simply to believe in these historical facts without truly receiving Christ as *your* Saviour. If this had been the scheme, then Christ had need only to come down and die; then go back to heaven and quietly wait to see who would believe the facts. But how different is the real case! Now Christ comes down to fill the soul with His own life and love. Penitent sinners hear and believe the truth concerning Jesus, and then receive Christ into the soul to live and reign there supreme and forever. On this point many mistake, saying, If I believe the facts as matters of history it is enough. *No!* No! This is not by any means. *'With the heart* man believeth unto righteousness.' The atonement was indeed made to provide the way so that Jesus could come down to human hearts and draw them into union and sympathy with Himself - so that God could let down the arms of His love and embrace sinners - so that law and government should not be dishonoured by such tokens of friendship shown by God toward sinners. But the atonement will by no means save sinners only as it prepares the way for them to come into sympathy and fellowship of heart with God.

Now Jesus comes to each sinner's door and knocks. Hark! what's that? what's that? Why this knocking? Why did He not go away and stay in heaven if that were the system, till men should simply believe the historical facts and be baptised, as some suppose, for salvation. But now Jesus, see how He comes down - tells the sinner what He has done - reveals all His love - tells him how holy and sacred it is, so sacred that He can by no means act without reference to the holiness of His law and the purity of His government. Thus impressing on the heart the most deep and enlarged ideas of His holiness and purity, He enforces the need of deep repentance and the sacred duty of renouncing all sin.

REMARKS

1. **The Bible teaches that sinners may forfeit their birthright and put themselves beyond the reach of mercy.** It is not long since I made some remarks to you on the manifest necessity

that God should guard Himself against the abuses of His love. The circumstances are such as create the greatest danger of such abuse, and, therefore, He must make sinners know that they may not abuse His love, and cannot do it with impunity.

2. **Under the Gospel, sinners are in circumstances of the greatest possible responsibility.** They are in the utmost danger of trampling down beneath their feet the very Son of God. Come, they say, let us kill Him and the inheritance shall be ours. When God sends forth, last of all, His own beloved Son, what do they do? Add to all their other sins and rebellions the highest insult to this glorious Son! Suppose something analogous to this were done under a human government. A case of rebellion occurs in some of the provinces. The King sends his own son, not with an army, to cut them down quick in their rebellion, but all gently, meekly, patiently, he goes among them, explaining the laws of the kingdom and exhorting them to obedience. What do they do in the case? With one consent they combine to seize him and put him to death!

But you deny the application of this, and ask me. Who murdered the Son of God? Were they not Jews? Aye, and have you, sinners, had no part in this murder? Has not your treatment of Jesus Christ shown that you are most fully in sympathy with the ancient Jews in their murder of the Son of God? If you had been there, would any one have shouted louder that you, Away with Him - crucify Him, crucify Him? Have you not always said, Depart from us - for we desire not the knowledge of Thy ways?

3. **It was said of Christ that, Though rich, He became poor that we through His poverty might be rich.** How strikingly true is this! Our redemption cost Christ His life; it found Him rich, but made Him poor; it found us infinitely poor, but made us rich even to all the wealth of heaven. But of these riches none can partake till they shall each for himself accept them in the legitimate way. They must be received on the terms proposed, or the offer passes utterly away, and you are left

poorer even than if no such treasures have ever been laid at your feet.

Many persons seem entirely to misconceive this case. They seem not to believe what God says, but keep saying, *If, if, if* there only were any salvation for me - *if* there were only an atonement provided for the pardon for my sins. This was one of the last things that was cleared up in my mind before I fully committed my soul to trust God. I had been studying the atonement; I saw its philosophical bearings - saw what it demanded of the sinner; but it irritated me, and I said - If I should become a Christian, how could I know what God would do with me? Under this irritation I said foolish and bitter things against Christ - till my own soul was horrified at its own wickedness, and I said - I will make all this up with Christ if the thing is possible.

In this way many advance upon the encouragements of the Gospel as if it were only a peradventure, and *experiment*. They take each forward step most carefully, with fear and trembling, as if there were the utmost doubt whether there could be any mercy for them. So with myself. I was on my way to my office, when the question came before my mind - What are you waiting for? You need not get up such an ado. All is done already. You have only to consent to the proposition - give your heart right up to it at once - this is all. Just so it is. All Christians and sinners ought to understand that the whole plan is complete - that the whole of Christ - His character, His work, His atoning death, and His ever-living intercession - belong to each and every man, and need only to be accepted. *There* is a full ocean of it. There it is. You may just as well take it as not. It is as if you stood on the shore of an ocean of soft, pure water, famishing with thirst; you are welcome to drink, and you need not fear lest you exhaust that ocean, or starve anybody else by drinking yourself. You need not feel that you are not made free to that ocean of waters; you are invited and pressed to drink - yea, to *drink abundantly!* This ocean supplies all your need. You do not need to have in yourself the attributes of Jesus Christ, for His attributes become practically yours for all possible use. As saith the Scripture - He is of God made unto us wisdom, righteousness, sanctification, and redemption. What do you need? Wisdom? Here it is. Righteousness? Here it is. Sanctification? Here you have it. All is in Christ. Can you possibly think of any one thing needful for your moral purity, or your usefulness which is not here in Christ? Nothing. All is provided here. Therefore you need not say, I will go and pray and try, as the hymn-

'I'll go to Jesus tho' my sin
Hath like a mountain rose,
Perhaps He will admit my plea;
Perhaps will hear my prayer.'

There is no need of any *perhaps*. The doors are always open. Like the doors of Broadway Tabernacle in New York, made to swing open and fasten themselves open, so that they could not swing back and shut down upon the crowds of people thronging to pass through. When they were to be made, I went myself to the workmen and told them by all means to fix them so that they must swing open and fasten themselves in that position.

So the door of salvation is open always - fastened open, and no man can shut it - not the Pope, even, nor the devil, nor any angel from heaven or from hell. There it stands, all swung back and the passage wide open for every sinner of our race to enter if he will.

Again, sin is the most expensive thing in the universe. Are you well aware, O sinner, what a price has been paid for you that you may be redeemed and made an heir of God and of heaven? O what an expensive business for you to indulge in sin!

And what an enormous tax the government of God has paid to redeem this province from its ruin! Talk about the poor tax of Great Britain and of all other nations superadded; all is nothing to the sin-tax of Jehovah's government - that awful *sin-tax!* Think how much machinery is kept in motion to save sinners! The Son of God was sent down - angels are sent as ministering spirits to the heirs of salvation; missionaries are sent, Christians labour, and pray, and weep in deep and anxious solicitude - all to seek and save the lost. What a wonderful - enormous tax is levied upon the benevolence of the universe to put away sin and to save the sinner! If the cost could be computed in solid gold, what a world of it - a solid globe of itself! What an array of toil and cost, from angels, Jesus Christ, the Divine Spirit, and living men! Shame on sinners who hold on to sin despite of all these benevolent efforts to save them! who instead of being ashamed out of sin, will say - Let God pay off this tax; who cares! Let the missionaries labour, let pious women work their very fingers off to raise funds to keep all this human machinery in motion; no matter: what is all this to me? I have loved my pleasures and after them I will go! What an unfeeling heart is this!

Sinners can very well afford to make sacrifices to save their fellow sinners. Paul could for his fellow sinners. He felt that he had done his part toward making sinners, and now it became him to do his part also in converting them back to God. But see there - that young man thinks he cannot afford to be a minister, for he is afraid he shall not be well supported. Does he not owe something to the grace that saved his soul from hell? Has he not some sacrifices to make, since Jesus has made so many for him, and Christians too, in Christ before him - did they not pray and suffer and toil for his salvation? As to his danger of lacking bread in the Lord's work, let him trust his Great Master. Yet let me also say that churches may be in great fault for not comfortably supporting their pastors. Let them know God will assuredly starve them if they starve their ministers. Their own souls and the souls of their children shall be barren as death if they avariciously starve those whom God in His providence sends to feed them with the bread of life.

How much it costs to rid society of certain forms of sin, as for example, *slavery*. How much has been expended already, and how much more yet remains to be expended ere this sore evil and curse and sin shall be rooted from our land! This is part of God's great enterprise, and He will press it on to its completion. Yet at what an amazing cost! How many lives and how much agony to get rid of this one sin!

Woe to those who make capital out of the sins of men! Just think of the rumseller - tempting men while God is trying to dissuade them from rushing on in the ways of sin and death! Think of the guilt of those who thus set themselves in array against God! So Christ has to contend with rumsellers who are doing all they can to hinder His work.

Our subject strikingly illustrates the nature of sin as mere selfishness. It cares not how much sin costs Jesus Christ - how much it costs the Church, and how much it taxes the benevolent sympathies and the self-sacrificing labours of all the good in earth or heaven; - no matter; the sinner loves self-indulgence and will have it while he can. How many of you have cost your friends countless tears and trouble to get you back from your ways of sin? Are you not ashamed when so much has been done for you, that you cannot be persuaded to give up your sins and turn to God and holiness?

The whole effort on the part of God for man is one of suffering and self-denial. Beginning with the sacrifice of His own beloved Son, it is carried on with ever renewed sacrifices and toilsome labours - at great and wonderful expense. Just think how long a *time* these efforts have been protracted already - how many tears, poured out like water, it has cost - how much *pain* in many forms this enterprise has caused and cost - yea, that very sin which you roll as a sweet morsel under your tongue! God may well hate it when He sees how much it costs, and say - O do not that abominable thing that I hate!

Yet God is not unhappy in these self-denials. So great is His joy in the results, that He deems all the suffering but comparatively a trifle, even as earthly parents enjoy the efforts they make to bless their children. See them; they will almost work their very hands off; - mothers sit up at night to ply their needle till they reel with fatigue and blindness; but if you were to see their toil, you would often see also their joy, so intensely do they love their children.

Such is the labour, the joy, and the self-denial of the Father, the Son, and the Holy Ghost, in their great work for human salvation. Often are they grieved that so many will refuse to be saved. Toiling on in a common sympathy, there is nothing, within reasonable limits, which they will not do or suffer to accomplish their great work. It is wonderful to think how all creation sympathises, too, in this work and its necessary sufferings. Go back to the scene of Christ's sufferings. Could the sun in the heavens look down unmoved on such a scene? O no, he could not even behold it - but veiled his face from the sight! All nature seemed to put on her robes of deepest mourning. The scene was too much for even inanimate nature to bear. The sun turned his back and could not look down on such a spectacle!

The subject illustrates forcibly the worth of the soul. Think you God would have done all this if He had had those low views on this subject which sinners usually have?

Martyrs and saints enjoy their sufferings - filling up in themselves what is lacking of the sufferings of Christ; not in the atonement proper, but in the subordinate parts of the work to be done. It is the nature of true religion to love self-denial.

The results will fully justify all the expense. God had well counted the cost before He began. Long time before He formed a moral universe He knew perfectly what it must cost Him to redeem sinners, and He knew that the result would amply justify all the cost. He knew that a wonder of mercy would be wrought - that the suffering demanded of Christ, great as it was, would be endured; and that results infinitely glorious would accrue therefrom. He looked down the track of time into the distant ages - where, as the cycles rolled along, there might be seen the joys of redeemed saints, who are singing their songs and striking their harps anew with the everlasting song, through the long, *long*, LONG eternity of their blessedness; - and was not this enough for the heart of infinite love to enjoy? And what do you think of it, Christian? Will you say now, I am ashamed to ask to be forgiven? How can I bear to receive such mercy! It is the price of blood, and how can I accept it? How can I make Jesus Christ so much expense?

You are right in saying that you have cost Him great expense - but the expense has been cheerfully met - the pain has all been endured, and will not need to be endured again, and it will cost none the more if you accept than if you decline; and moreover still, let it be considered, Jesus Christ has not acted unwisely; He did not pay too much for the soul's redemption - not a pang more than the interests of God's government demanded and the worth of the soul would justify.

O, when you come to see Him face to face, and tell Him what you think of it - when you are some thousands of years older than you are now, will you not adore that wisdom that manages this scheme, and the infinite love in which it had its birth? O what will you then say of that amazing condescension that brought down Jesus to your rescue! Say, Christian, have you not often poured out your soul before your Saviour in acknowledgement of what you have cost Him, and there seemed to be a kind of lifting up as if the very bottom of your soul were to rise and you would pour out your whole heart. If anybody had seen you they would have wondered what had happened to you that you had so melted your soul in gratitude and love.

Say now, sinner, will you sell your birthright? How much will you take for it? How much will you take for your interest in Christ? For how much will you sell your soul? Sell your Christ! Of old they sold Him for thirty pieces of silver; and ever since, the heavens have been raining tears of blood on our guilty world. If you were to be asked by the devil to fix the sum for which you would sell your soul, what would be the price named? Lorenzo Dow once met a man as he was riding along a solitary road to fulfil an appointment, and said to him - Friend have you ever prayed? No. How much will you take to *never* pray hereafter? One dollar. Dow paid it over and rode on. The man put the money in his pocket, and passed on, *thinking*. The more he thought the worse he felt. There, said he, I have sold my soul for one dollar! It must be that I have met the *devil!* Nobody else would tempt me so. With all my soul I must repent or be damned forever!

How often have you bargained to sell your Saviour for less than thirty pieces of silver! Nay, for the merest trifle!

Finally God wants volunteers to help on this great work God has given Himself, and given His Son, and sent His Spirit but more labourers are still needed; and what will you give? Paul said, I bear in my body the marks of the Lord Jesus. Do you aspire such an honour? What will you do - what will you suffer? Say not, I have nothing to give. You can give yourself - your eyes, your ears, your hands, your mind, your heart, all; and surely nothing you have is too sacred and too good to be devoted to such a work upon such a call! How many young men are ready to go? and how many young women? Whose heart leaps up crying - Here am I! send me!

REV. ROBERT L. MOYER, D.D.

D r. Moyer, whose father was a saloonkeeper, was himself a drunkard before being saved from a life of sin. Following his conversion he began studying at Moody Bible Institute, and then became engaged in evangelistic ministry from 1915-1920. He then received a call to be pastor of the United Brethren Church in Minneapolis, and then for twenty years he was a teacher of Bible in Northwestern Bible and Missionary Training School and Seminary.

Later Dr. W.B. Riley invited him to become his assistant at First Baptist Church in Minneapolis and when Dr. Riley retired in 1942, Dr. Moyer then became pastor and served in that capacity until his death.

Dr. Harry Ironside said of Dr. Moyer: 'Few men have the winsomeness and tenderness, combined with sound scriptural teaching, that characterises the ministry of my esteemed friend and fellow labourer, Dr. Robert Moyer.'

Dr. Moyer published several books including *Love So Amazing, Meditations in Isaiah Fifty-Three*, and *John 3:16* - a series of ten sermons on the greatest text of the Bible.

This sermon *His Only Begotten Son* was first published in 1938.

5

HIS ONLY BEGOTTEN SON

The story is told of a child who had been taught to think of God only with dread, as of a terrible judge. In her stern home the name of God had been mentioned only to terrify and frighten her. One day, in her father's printing office, she picked up a scrap of paper and found on it the first words of this verse, 'God so loved the world that He gave'. The remaining words were torn off, but even in this mere fragment there was a revelation to her. It told her that God loved the world, loved it well enough to give something. What He gave she did not know, but it was a great deal for Him to give anything to it. The new thought brought great joy to her heart. It changed all her conceptions of God. She learned to think of Him as One Who loved her, as her Friend, ready to give her rich gifts and all good, and this thought brightened and transformed her life.

We know what God gave - His only begotten Son. How much greater should be our conception of God, our joy of heart, the brightness of our life in the light of the unspeakable Gift.

'HIS ONLY BEGOTTEN SON' DEFINES CHRIST'S ETERNAL RELATIONSHIP.

We must remember that the word 'son' in Scripture is a word of relationship, not necessarily one of origin. David was the son of Saul - by relationship (1 Samuel 26:21,25). In Matthew 1:16 Joseph is the son of Jacob; in Luke 3:23 he is the son of Heli. One man cannot have two fathers, yet both statements are true. Joseph was the son of Jacob by birth; he was the son of Heli by relationship, that is, by marriage.

Christ's sonship is a relationship within the Godhead. As Hodge says, in commenting on the Trinity, 'The First Person is called Father, not because of His relation to His creatures, but because of His relation to the Second Person. The Second Person is called Son, not because of any relation assumed in time, but because of His eternal relation to the First Person.'

In human relationships we say 'father' of one who existed before a son was born. Remember, however, that he did not become father until a son was born. The one who believes in an eternal Father but not in an eternal Son must explain how we can have a father without a son. One who has no son is not a father; therefore, since God the Father is eternally existing, God the Son is eternally existing. There never has been a time when the Father did not exist as the Father. The Son always has been and always will be the Son.

The words Father, Son, and Spirit indicate eternal distinctions in the Godhead. We have no more right to say that the Son was created than we have to say that the Father had a beginning. God is God. He always has been God. He is immutable; that is, unchangeable. This immutability refers to His nature, not to His operations. God is absolutely perfect. Perfection does not admit of change. There has never been a time when God has not been manifested as a Trinity. The words Father, Son, and Spirit indicate *eternal* distinctions in the Godhead. The one who holds that there was a time that Jesus Christ was not the Son of God involves the Godhead in such a stupendous change as to practically demolish God. But the Godhead is unchangeable. There are different times and manners of manifestation of God, but there is no difference in the Godhead. The Son is co-existent, co-equal, co-eternal, co-essential with the Father.

Since God is eternal and the Son is His only begotten Son; therefore, Jesus Christ is the eternally begotten Son of God. A begotten son is one who partakes of the essence of the father. *The* Son partakes of the essence of *the* Father, and so is the eternally begotten of the Father.

I know it is practically impossible to understand eternal generation. Someone has tried to help in the understanding by the use of the sun. The sun is continually generating light. The very instant it dropped from God's creative lips it began to generate light. The light of the sun is as old as the sun itself. You have light the instant you have the sun. The sun had a beginning. It will have an ending, but had it never had a beginning, and if it should never have an ending, then you would have the eternal generation of light. God is eternal, and Jesus Christ is the eternally begotten of God.

The Fatherhood in eternity became the Fatherhood in time when Christ came into this world by way of the virgin birth. Please remember that when we speak of the virgin birth we are speaking of the manner by which God became incarnate. We are not talking about the mere birth of a baby. 'God was manifest in the flesh'. We believe that God always manifests Himself through the Second Person of the Trinity, hence, God manifest in the flesh is called the Son of God. Jesus Christ was neither a descendant of God nor a descendant of man. He is God. Sacred prophecy speaks of Christ's incarnation as that of 'the child born,' 'the son given' (Isaiah 9:6). To transpose 'son' and 'child' is to create confusion. As the Son, He was not born, but given. As the Child, He was not given, but born. He did not receive a personality from the Father in heaven; He did not owe His manhood to a father on earth. The Spirit of God formed within Mary a body through which God took a human nature into union with His Divine personality. In nature He was God-man; in personality He was God. It will help if we bear in mind the fact that we do not have three Gods, but one God Who is a Unity in Trinity and a Trinity in Unity. The Father alone is not God, the Son alone is not God, the Spirit alone is not God, but all three constitute God, for

God is Father, Son, and Spirit. You cannot have one Person of the Godhead without having the other two; hence, it is written concerning Christ that 'in Him dwelleth all the fullness of the Godhead bodily'; that is, in a human body. Christ was God manifest in the flesh.

He was announced to Mary as the Son of God. 'That holy thing that shall be born of thee shall be called the Son of God' (Luke 1:35).

He was announced to Mary as Saviour. 'Thou shalt conceive in thy womb and bring forth a Son, and shall call His name Jesus - for He shall save His people from their sins' (Luke 1:31; Matthew 1:21). 'For there is one God, and one mediator between God and men, the man Christ Jesus; Who gave Himself a ransom for all' (1 Timothy 2:5-6). Westcott points out that the word 'between' would be better rendered 'partaker'; that is, 'partaker of God and man,' meaning that He partakes the nature of the two parties. The same word in Hebrews 7:2 is translated 'part'. Jesus Christ is unique. He is truly a Being by Himself. He stands alone in the eternal sonship in His past Being. He stands alone in His sonship as born alone to die for our sins.

The very title 'Son of God' marks His equality with God. The Jews knew very well what He meant when He claimed to be the Son of God. 'Therefore, the Jews sought the more to kill Him, because He not only had broken the sabbath, but said also that God was His Father, making Himself equal with God' (John 5:18).

It is very instructive to note that the Lord Jesus was recognised by the only beings who had ever seen Him before His entrance into the world. When the eyes of that other world looked upon Him, they cried out, 'Thou art the Son of God.'

Some maintain that He is the Son of God by miraculous conception. This is not true. He was the Son of God before that human birth. He is so named in Psalm 2.

Some declare that He is the Son of God by appointment to office. John 10:36 is introduced for proof. 'Say ye of him, whom the Father hath sanctified, and sent into the world, Thou blasphemest; because I said, I am the Son of God?' This verse, however, does not teach that He became Son by being sent, but, being the Son of God, He was sent.

Some affirm that He is the Son of God by the resurrection of the dead. 'God hath fulfilled the same unto us their children, in that He hath raised up Jesus again; as it is also written in the second Psalm, Thou art My Son, this day have I begotten Thee' (Acts 13:33). This meaning of the resurrection is made clearer, however, from Romans 1:4, which states that He was declared to be the Son by resurrection - not that He became the Son by resurrection. 'Declared to be' means marked out, determined. Christ's resurrection forever settled the question of His sonship. The voice from heaven at the baptism and again at the transfiguration said, 'This is My Son.' The resurrection had not yet occurred.

Some insist that He is the Son of God only because He was made Heir of all things (Hebrews 1:3-5), but sonship does not come from heirship; heirship comes from sonship. Abraham recognised this, for he said, 'Lo, one born in my house is mine heir.'

Jesus Christ is the 'only' Son of God. Angels are called sons of God, and such they are by creation. Adam was called a son of God, and such he was by creation. Believers are called sons of God, and such they are by regeneration. But Jesus Christ is the only Son of God. He is the Isaac of His Father (Genesis 22:2; 25:5). Jesus Christ was the Son in eternity; we become sons in time. He was the Son by eternal generation; we become the sons by faith. He was of the same essence with the Father; we are of different substance from the Father. He is called THE Son, distinguished from all others. He is not A Son. Napoleon Bonaparte once said, 'I know men, and I tell you Jesus Christ is not a mere man. He is truly a Being by Himself.'

F. E. Marsh says that at one time in a conversation with a sea captain in the town of Sunderland, the captain said, 'I cannot believe that Jesus is the Son of God. He never claimed to be.'

Marsh replied, 'Would you believe that Jesus is the Son of God if He claimed to be?'

'Yes,' was the reply.

Marsh said, 'Christ once asked His disciples about Himself, "Whom do men say that I, the Son of Man, am?"'

'What did they say?'

'They gave various answers, but Peter said, "Thou art the Christ, the Son of the living God."'

'What did Christ say in reply?'

'"Blessed art thou Simon Bar-Jona, for flesh and blood hath not revealed in unto thee, but My Father which is in heaven."'

That was sufficient for the captain, for he clasped his hands and said, 'Oh, Christ, Thou Son of God, I acknowledge Thy deity, and pray Thee to save me because Thou didst die for me on Calvary's Cross.'

'HIS ONLY BEGOTTEN SON' DESCRIBES GOD'S SUPREME GIFT

This gift is the Son of God. No other son would do. Not Joseph's son. He was addressed as the son of Joseph by the people of Nazareth (Luke 4:22), even as some today call Him the son of Joseph. He was so addressed because that was what they believed, but if He were the son of Joseph, He was conceived in iniquity and born in sin, and could not be a Saviour. He, Himself, would then have needed a Saviour; would have needed to be born again. That would mean that His mother was stained with the sin of unchastity and just as guilty as a wife who breaks her marriage vow. That would mean that He had no legal, no decent right to live, but was a bastard, born out of wedlock. That would mean that He was not the Second Person of the Trinity, and if He is not the Second Person of the Trinity, there is no Second Person of the Trinity, hence there is no Trinity. A denial of any Person of the Godhead is a denial of God. The son of Joseph could not forgive sins. The son of Joseph could no more sacrifice for my sins than you could.

Sin required a victim since God is just. 'Where is the lamb?' said Isaac, and Abraham answered, 'My son, God will provide Himself a lamb,' and God provided His only begotten Son. No other son is ever called the Lamb of God.

It is a hard thing to give a son. During a famine in Germany centuries ago, a poor family being ready to perish, the husband proposed to the wife that they sell one of their children for bread to relieve themselves and the rest. Finally, the mother consented to do so. Then they began to think about which one of the four should be sold. They named the eldest, but they both refused to part with that one - he was the first born. Well, they came to the second, but they could not part with him, for he was the very picture and image of his father. Then they talked about the third one, but that one looked most like the mother, and they could not part with that one. Only one left, and that was the baby. He was the Benjamin, the last born. They couldn't sell him, so they determined that they would rather perish than part with one of their children. Remember how Jacob mourned when Joseph and Benjamin were rent from him. What is a child but a piece of the parent wrapped up in another skin? To give a child is like giving your own heart and being. And yet our dearest children are but strangers to us in comparison to the unspeakable dearness between the Father and Christ.

The hardest thing the writer ever did was to say one morning, thirteen years ago when his only son was dying, 'All right, Father, take him.' How hard to give him up! And yet, to what was I giving him? To hands of love. To the glory of heaven. Then stop to think to what God gave His only Son - to sin, to degradation, to curse, to death, to judgement. The greatest manifestation of love in the whole universe is in that gift of God's Son for us. Just think how precious to Him you must be in the light of the gift of His Son for you.

'HIS ONLY BEGOTTEN SON' DISCHARGES GOD'S SAVING PURPOSE

As soon as sin entered the world God declared His purpose to send a Redeemer (Genesis 3:15). That Redeemer was to be the Seed of the woman Whose redeeming death was indicated in the crushed heel.

In 1 John 4:14 it is very definitely and distinctly stated that the Father sent His Son to be the Saviour of the world. In Galatians 4:4-6 we are told that God sent forth His Son to redeem. In Romans 8:32, we are told that God spared not His own Son, but gave Him up to death for us all. In 1 John 4:10 we are told that God sent His Son to be the propitiation or satisfaction for our sins.

It was for this purpose that He came down from heaven. But for Calvary there would have been no Bethlehem. He was born that He might die. The expression 'Mine hour' is found seven times in John's gospel. That hour is the hour of His death. That is the greatest hour since hours began to be numbered. The hour of His resurrection was only God's approval upon the hour of His death. That was the hour fixed by the triune God even before the foundation of the world. That was the hour which, in the eternal councils of the Godhead, had been marked out for the sacrificial work and death of the Son of God. It was for the sake of that hour that He left the bosom of the Father for the womb of the virgin. That was the hour when the seed of the serpent bruised the heel of the Seed of the woman. That was the hour that God had in mind when He clad Adam and Eve in coats of skin. That was the hour in which Abel had hope as he offered the firstling of the flock to God. That was the hour which Abraham saw as he looked away from the altar on Mount Moriah where his own son was ready to be offered. 'Abraham rejoiced to see My day,' the Lord said. That was the hour that gave value to the blood of the passover lamb. The thousands of Israelites came with their droves of beasts for the altar of Jehovah, but now the fire is quenched, the altar is hewn down, the sacrifices are driven away, for the hour of which they speak is now fulfilled. The Holy of Holies was aglow with the divine Shekinah. The great High Priest was there. Israel stood without confessing her sins. The sacrificial victims were bleeding. But now - the veil of the temple, rent from the top throughout, is left fluttering in the winds of heaven. The Holiest is deserted. Why? Because the hour of which they spoke is fulfilled in Calvary. The brazen serpent on the pole pointed off to that hour. The smitten rock was only the shadow of the smitten Redeemer. Psalm 22, with its pierced, suffering, dying Man who cried, 'My God, my God, why hast Thou forsaken Me?' is meaningless apart from that hour. Isaiah wrote of that hour, 'He was wounded for our transgressions, He was bruised for our iniquities.' 'The Lord hath laid on Him the iniquity of us all.' Zechariah had that hour in view when he cried out, 'Awake, O sword against my shepherd, and against the man that is my fellow' (Zechariah 13:7). All the prophecies, all the types, all the shadows, all the symbols met at the Cross in that hour, and the end of them all came with that last loud cry that sent its echoes pealing through the plains of Judea - 'It is finished!' That was the hour when the One without sin was made to be sin for us, when He bare our sins in His own body on the tree. That was the hour to which the prophets pointed. That is the hour to which we now look. It is the hour to which all ages point and to which all dispensations look. That was the hour when the new covenant was sealed and our salvation secured in the blood of the Son of God.

He said, 'The Son of Man must be lifted up.' 'Must' means 'must'. None other could fulfil the saving purpose of God because He alone is the Son of God. He alone is sinless, and so He alone could bear our sins.

A missionary, in charge of one of the native churches in China, was examining a number of candidates for Christian baptism. He asked a woman who had applied for church membership, 'Had Jesus sin?' and somewhat to the missionary's astonishment, although she had been taught otherwise, she replied, 'Yes.' The missionary thought that perhaps she did not understand the question, and so repeated it in a way likely to elicit a negative reply, but the woman answered very positively, 'He had sin.' Then the missionary asked her if she did not understand that the Lord Jesus was God incarnate and could have no sin, but her unhesitating reply was, 'Why He had mine.' That woman seemed to be a deeper theologian than the missionary himself. She knew that the Lord had laid on Him the iniquity of us all, and that He bare our sins in His own body on the tree.

'All thy sins were laid upon Him,
Jesus bore them on the tree;
God, who knew them, laid them on Him,
And, believing, thou art free.'

'HIS ONLY BEGOTTEN SON' DETERMINES MAN'S ETERNAL DESTINY

'He that believeth on the Son hath everlasting life; and he that believeth not the Son shall not see life; but the wrath of God abideth on him' (John 3:36).

It is to as many as received Him that He gives power to become the sons of God, even to them who believe on His name. John 1:12 makes it plain that receiving and believing are synonymous terms. The one who believes on the Lord Jesus Christ is the one who receives Him as a personal Saviour.

A friend of mine recently received a gift from one with whom he was not in fellowship. He immediately returned the gift to the one who sent it. He refused to receive it. In like manner men may refuse God's great Gift of His only begotten Son. Such a refusal means no life, but only the wrath of God. On the other hand, to receive God's Gift means a place in God's family with the eternal privileges and blessings that shall be the portion of every child of God. So man's destiny is sealed by his acceptance or rejection of Jesus Christ as Saviour.

Dr. George F. Pentecost tells the story of a poor ragged little Scotch girl who came to him one night in Aberdeen, after nearly all the other people had gone out from the service, and followed him about as he was leaving the hall. Finally, he asked her what she wanted. He fully expected that she was a little beggar; and so she was, but it was the Bread of Life she was after. 'Lassie,' he said, 'what do you want?' The little girl reached up on her tiptoes as he bent down, and whispered into his ear, 'I want to get saved.' He was surprised and startled at the intensity of her whispered words, and drew back and looked her eagerly in the face, and repeated her own words for answer, 'You want to get saved?' 'Ay, sir, I do,' ever so pathetically, and still in a whisper. 'And why do you want to get saved?' Again on her tiptoes she reached up and whispered in his ear, 'Because I am a sinner.' This was so satisfactory a reason, and by this time the child had so interested him that he drew her to one side, away from the gentlemen who were standing by, that he might talk with her unreservedly. 'How do you know you are a sinner? Who told you so?' 'Because God says so in the Book; and I feel it right here,' and she laid her little hand on her breast, as the publican did when he said, 'God be merciful to me a sinner.' 'Well,' said Dr. Pentecost, 'do you think I can save you?' Up to this time she had spoken in whispers; but now drawing away from him her eyes taking fire, her words rang out short and clear, 'No, no, man; you cannot save me. No man can save a sinner.' By this his interest was greatly deepened, and he drew her down beside him on one of the benches, and taking her little hand in his, and speaking as kindly as he knew how, he said to her, 'You are quite right; no man can save you, much less I. Tell me why, then, did you come to me? I cannot save you. Who, then, can save you?' Again she dropped into a whisper, and almost touched his ear with her lips. There was an infinite pathos in her voice as she said, 'Jesus can save me.' 'Yes, you are quite right. Jesus can save you. But tell me how can He save you? What has He done to save you?' Again the lips to his ear, and again the eager whisper - if possible more pathetic and tender, 'Oh, sir, He died for me.' Out of curiosity to know how the little waif, who had so hotly repudiated the idea of man's ability to save, would answer, Dr. Pentecost replied, 'Then He is dead, is He? How can He save you if He is dead?' The little thing sprang up from her seat, and her eyes, only a moment before suffused with tears, flashed upon him. No whisper now, no timid putting of lips to his ear, but her voice rang out as once before, 'He is not dead. He is not dead!' 'But you just now said that He died for you. If He died for you He must be dead. How can a dead man save you, however good and loving He may have been?' She looked at him as in amazement, and lifting her little lean bare arm as in striking gesture she replied again, 'Man, Jesus is not dead. He died for me, but He is not a dead Man. He is God's Son. Man, did you not tell us this very night that God raised Him from the dead? He was dead, but He is not dead now. Oh, man, I want to get saved!' and her voice dropped into the old pathetic tones. 'Do not fool me, but tell me all about it, and how I can get saved.' He had preached that night from the text, 'He was delivered for our offences, and raised again for our justification.' And this little waif had been drinking it in. He did tell her all about it, and she went away glad and thankful, and full of the consciousness that her sins were forgiven by the Saviour Who was alive forevermore.

ARTHUR TAPPAN PIERSON

Arthur Tappan Pierson was born in New York City in 1837. He graduated from Union Theological Seminary in 1860 and was ordained by the Presbyterian Church. After serving various congregations in America he came to London and preached in the Metropolitan Tabernacle, while Pastor C. H. Spurgeon was recovering from ill health. He eventually replaced Spurgeon as the pastor of the Tabernacle.

He wrote more than fifty books, and served for over twenty years as editor of the *Missionary Review*. He supported the Keswick movement's emphasis on personal holiness, and as a premillennialist promoted Christ's second coming as a motivation for spreading the gospel. He also contributed to *The Fundamentals* and was the first editor of the *Schofield Reference Bible*.

This sermon is taken from his book *The Heart Of The Gospel* and was preached in the Metropolitan Tabernacle in the autumn of 1891.

6

THE HEART OF THE GOSPEL

For God so loved the world, that He gave His only begotten Son, that whosoever believeth in Him should not perish, but have everlasting life. John 3:16.

There is one text in the New Testament that has been preached from oftener than any other in the Bible. It has been the foundation of great revivals of religion, like that among the Tahitians; or that among the Telugus in India, where two thousand two hundred and twenty-two people were baptised in one day, nearly five thousand people in thirty days, and ten thousand people within ten months; and where, even during the year drawing to its close, nearly ten thousand more souls have been baptised. It is a wonderful text. Luther called it one of 'the little gospels'. It is this (John 3:16) - 'For God so loved the world, that He gave His only begotten Son, that whosoever believeth in Him should not perish, but have everlasting life.'

You will naturally wonder what there is in that old text that is new. I have found something that was very new to me, and which may also be to you. I suppose that I had read that verse tens of thousands of times, and yet, a little while ago, as I was led to preach upon that text, I sought of the Lord a clearer view of it, that I might glorify Him, by bringing forth out of His treasure things new and old. After reading these familiar words over, perhaps a hundred times, prayerfully asking for new light and insight, there suddenly came to me this absolutely new discovery, as though one, looking up into the heavens, should see a cloud swept away from before the stars, and a new constellation revealed. It flashed on my thought that there are *ten words* in the verse that are quite prominent words, such as 'God,' 'loved,' 'world,' 'whosoever,' and so on. Then a little more close and careful search showed those words in a hitherto undiscovered mutual relation: *the ten words were in five pairs.* There is one pair of words that has to do with the two persons of the Godhead - God the Father, and God the Son. There is a second pair of words that has to do with the expression of the Father's attitude or posture towards this world - He 'loved,' and He 'gave.' Then there is a third pair of words that refers to the objects of the divine love - 'world,' and 'whosoever.' Then there is a fourth pair of words that shows us what the attitude of man ought to be when God's love and gift come to his knowledge - 'believe,' and 'have.' Then the last pair of words points us to the extremes of human destiny: the result of rejection, and the result of acceptance - 'perish,' and 'life.'

Often as I had read this 'gospel in a sentence,' I had never seen before that singular relation borne by the main words in the sentence; and, so far as I know, nobody else had seen it before; for it is one of the beautiful privileges about the study of the precious Word of God that the humblest believer who asks the grace of God and the guidance of the Holy Spirit in studying the holy Scriptures, may make a discovery for himself that nobody has ever made before, or if so, without his knowledge; so that it is still his own discovery.

Let us look at this text in the light of this fresh arrangement of the thoughts which it contains. To my mind, it is one of the most remarkable discoveries that it has ever been permitted me to make in the study and exploration of the hidden treasures of the Word of God.

THE FIRST PAIR OF WORDS - 'GOD' AND 'SON'

In the first place, '*God* so loved the world, that He gave His only begotten *Son.*' There are two of the persons of the Godhead. Many persons are troubled about the relation of the Father to the Son, and of the Son to the Father. They cannot exactly see how Jesus Christ can be equal with God if He is God's Son; and they cannot see how He can be as glorious as the Father, and how He can be entitled to the same honour and homage and worship as the Father if He proceeds forth from the Father, and comes into the world. But let us seek a simple illustration. It is said, in the introduction of this Gospel according to John. 'In the beginning was the Word, and the Word was with God, and the Word was God.' What is a word? It is the expression of a thought that lies in the mind. The thought is not visible, the thought is not audible; but, when it takes the form of a spoken word or a written word, that thought that was invisible in the mind, that you could not see, or hear, or know about in any other way, comes to your eye on the printed page, or to your ear through the voice of the speaker. And so my invisible thoughts are coming to you now through these audible words. The word is so connected with the thought that it is the expression of the thought. The thought is the word invisible: the word is the thought visible. Now Jesus Christ was the invisible thought of God put into a form in which you could see it and hear it; and just as the word and the thought are so connected that if you understand the word you understand the thought, and if you understand the thought you understand the word; and as the word would have no meaning without the thought, and the thought no expression without the word, so Jesus Christ helps us to understand the Father, and the Father could not make Himself perfectly known to us except through the Son. But, again, we are told that Christ is 'the Light of the world.' Suppose I should say, 'In the beginning was the light, and the light was with the sun, and the light was the sun.' The sun sends forth the light, and the light proceeds from the sun; yet the light and the sun are the same in nature and the same in essence, and the glory of the sun is the glory of the light, and the glory of the light is the glory of the sun; and although the light goes forth from the sun, it is equal with the sun, shares the same glory, and is entitled to the same valuation. We cannot think of one without the other.

In this text not a word is said about the love of the Son for sinners, nor a word about the Son's offering of Himself for the salvation of men. What is the common old-fashioned notion that we sometimes find cropping out even in the conceptions of Christian people, as well as unbelievers, in these days? Many think of the Father as representing justice, and of the Son as representing mercy. They imagine the Son as coming between the wrath of the Father and the guilty sinner. It is very much like the story of Pocahontas, the daughter of an Indian chief, who came between the executioner and Captain Smith, when the executioner was standing with his club uplifted, ready to strike the fatal blow on the head of his victim. The notion of a great many people is that God the Father is all wrath, and that we can never look at God or think of God, and that God never can look at us or think of us, except with a kind of mutual abhorrence and antagonism; and that so Jesus Christ incarnates the principle of love, and comes in between the angry God and the sinner. That is a very shallow notion indeed. Have you never got hold of the idea that the Father is just as much interested in you as the Son is, and that the Father loves you just as much as the Son does? Look at this verse. It puts all the glory of the love and the sacrifice upon the Father: '*God so loved* the world *that He gave* His only begotten Son.' He puts it thus that you and I may understand that our notion of the Son is our notion of the Father. When Philip said, 'Lord, show us the Father, and it sufficeth us,' Jesus answered, 'Have I been so long time with you, and yet hast thou not known me, Philip? he that hath seen Me hath seen the Father; and how sayest thou then, Shew us the Father?'

Do you not understand my thought if you understand my word? And if my word is the right expression of my thought, how absurd it would be for somebody to say, 'I understand his word well enough, but I wish that I could understand his thought.' My word, being human, may not always properly express my thought; but with God the Word is the perfect expression of the thought; and so if you have understood the word you have understood the thought: and if you have understood the thought you have understood the word. If you have seen the Son, you have seen the Father. If the love of the Son has touched you, the love of the Father has touched you. If you worship the Son, you worship the Father. If you obey the Son, you obey the Father; so that you need not be troubled about your feelings toward the Father, and say, as many a person has said to me, 'I wish that I could feel towards God the Father as I feel towards Jesus. I wish that I could have those views of God the Father that I have of Jesus. I wish that I could have the freedom with the Father that I have with the Son.'

Now, dismiss all that kind of trouble and perplexity from your mind; for as you think of the Son you think of the Father; as you love the Son, you love the Father; as you pray to the Son, you pray to the Father; and as you obey and serve the Son, you obey and serve the Father. The Son thinks of you just as the Father does, and the Father thinks of you just as the Son does.'

'So near, so very near to God,
Nearer I cannot be;
For in the person of His Son
I am as near as He.

So dear, so very dear to God,
Dearer I cannot be;
For the love wherewith He loves the Son
Is the love He bears to me.'

THE SECOND PAIR OF WORDS -
'LOVED' AND 'GAVE'

The second pair of words is 'loved' and 'gave.' He loved and gave. I have no desire to enter into nice distinctions, but with the simplicity of a little child approach this heart of the gospel. And yet a child will understand that when we use the word 'love,' we sometimes mean one thing and sometimes another. For instance, suppose that you should try to get some poor criminal out of prison - a miserable, filthy, degraded, defiled man. Somebody asks you why you do it, and you say that you *love* him. Now, that would not be taken to mean the same kind of love as you bear your mother. Those are very different loves - the love that you bear to your mother and the love that you bear to some vile criminal. The word 'love' has a different meaning in different cases. The apostle John says, 'We love Him because He first loved us.' Was not the love of God to us something different from the love that we bear to Him? I love God because I know Him to be the most beautiful, the most wise, the most glorious, the most fatherly, the most tender, the most pitiful, the most gracious Being in the universe. Why did He love me? Because He saw that I was beautiful and truthful, and lovely, and honest, and honourable? Not so, says the apostle. 'When we were enemies He loved us, and He commendeth His love toward us in that while we were yet sinners Christ died for us.' So there are two kinds of love. We call them the love of complacence and the love of benevolence. Complacence means a feeling of pleasure. You love a beautiful person, a lovely character, because you see something in the person and in the character that draws out your love. But that is not the kind of love that we call the love of benevolence, for such love is bestowed on people in whom we do not see anything beautiful or lovely. We love them for the sake of the good that we may do them, and for the sake of the beautiful character that, by grace, we may help to develop in them. So, therefore, the love of complacence is intensive, but the love of benevolence is extensive; the love of complacency is partial, the love of benevolence is impartial; the love of complacency is exclusive and select, the love of benevolence is inclusive and universal. The love of complacence is a kind of selfish love, but the love of benevolence is a generous love. The love of complacency may be an involuntary love: we see the qualities that attract affection, and we love unconsciously and involuntarily; but the love of benevolence is voluntarily exercised. The love of complacence has to do with comparatively few of the people whom we know; the love of benevolence takes in the whole world, and hundreds and thousands of people whom we do not know, and never saw, but whom, for the sake of Jesus, we love.

Have you fixed that in your thought? The kind of love, then, that God had for us was the love of benevolence - extensive, inclusive, impartial, universal, self-denying, self-forgetting, voluntary.

Now it is the characteristic of *that* kind of love that *it gives*. We call it the love of benevolence, and 'benevolence' is another word for 'giving'; and such love keeps nothing, but gives everything that it has, and gives to everybody. Of course, if God loved us after that sort He had to give. He could not so love if He did not give, any more than the sun could be the sun without shining, or a spring of water could be a spring without flowing out into a stream. And so these words, 'loved,' and 'gave,' naturally go together. You could not have the one without the other. There could not be this wonderful giving without this wonderful loving; and there could not be this wonderful loving without this wonderful giving.

THE THIRD PAIR OF WORDS - 'WORLD' AND 'WHOSOEVER'

Now let us look at the third pair of words - 'world,' and 'whosoever.'

It need not be said that these are both *universal terms*. 'World' is the most universal term that we have in the language. For instance, we sometimes mean by it the whole earth on which we dwell; sometimes the whole human family that dwells on the earth; and sometimes the world-age, or whole period during which the whole family of man occupies the sphere. That is the word that God uses to indicate the objects of His love. But there is always danger of our losing sight of ourselves in a multitude of people. In the great mass individuals are lost, and it becomes to us simply a countless throng. But when God looks at us, He never forgets each individual. Every one of you tonight stands out just as plainly before the Lord as though you were the only man, woman, or child on earth. So God adds here another word, 'whosoever,' that is also universal, but with this difference between the two: 'world' is collectively universal, that is, it takes all men in the mass; 'whosoever' is distributively universal, that is, it takes everyone out of the mass, and holds him up separately before the Lord. If this precious text only said, 'God so loved the world, that He gave His only begotten Son,' one might say, 'Oh, He never thought of me. He had a kind of general love to the whole world, but He never thought of me.' But when God uses that all-embracing word 'whosoever,' that must mean you and me; for whatever my name or yours may be, our name is 'whosoever,' is it not? John Newton used to say that it was a great deal better for him that this verse had the word 'whosoever' in it than the words 'John Newton'; 'for,' he said, 'if I read "God so loved the world, that He gave His only begotten Son, that when John Newton believed he should have everlasting life," I should say, perhaps, there is some other John Newton; but 'whosoever' means this John Newton and the other John Newton, and everybody else, whatever his name may be.' Blessed be the Lord! He would not have us forget that He thought of each one of us, and so He said, 'whosoever.' You notice the same thing in the great commission, 'Go ye into all the world' (collectively universal) ' and preach the gospel to every creature' (distributively universal).

Before I leave this pair of words, let me illustrate what a precious term this word 'whosoever' is. It reminds me of the great gates of this Tabernacle, that spring open to let in poor souls that want to hear the gospel. This word 'whosoever' is the wide gateway to salvation, and lets in any poor sinner who seeks to find for himself a suffering but reigning Saviour.

In the South Seas, in the beginning of the present century, was a man of the name of Hunt, who had gone to preach the gospel to the inhabitants of Tahiti. The missionaries had laboured there for about fourteen or fifteen years, but had not, as yet, a single convert. Desolating wars were then spreading across the island of Tahiti and the neighbouring islands. The most awful idolatry, sensuality, ignorance, and brutality, with everything else that was horrible prevailed; and the Word of God seemed to have made no impression upon those awfully degraded islanders. A translation of the gospel according to John had just been completed, and Mr. Hunt, before it was printed, read, from the manuscript translation, the third chapter; and, as he read on, he reached the sixteenth verse, and, in the Tahitian language, gave those poor idolaters this compact little gospel: 'God so loved the world, that He gave His only begotten Son, that whosoever believeth in Him should not perish, but have everlasting life.'

A chief stepped out from the rest (Pomare II), and said, 'Would you read that again, Mr. Hunt?' Mr. Hunt read it again. 'Would you read that once more?' and he read it once more. 'Ah!' said the man 'that may be true of you white folks, but it is not true of us down here in these islands. The gods have no such love as that for us.' Mr. Hunt stopped in his reading, and he took that one word 'whosoever,' and by it showed that poor chief that God's gospel message meant *him*: that it could not mean one man or woman any more than another. Mr. Hunt was expounding this wonderful truth, when Pomare II said, 'Well, then, if that is the case, your book shall be my book, and your God shall be my God, and your people shall be my people, and your heaven shall be my home. We, down on the island of Tahiti, never heard of any God that loved us and loved everybody in that way.' And that first convert is now the leader of a host, numbering nearly a million, in the South Seas. Reference has already been made to the fact that this was the great text that Dr. Clough found so blessed among the Telugus. When the great famine came on, in 1877, and the missionaries were trying to distribute relief among the people, Dr. Clough, who was a civil engineer, took a contract to complete the Buckingham Canal, and he got the famishing people to come in gangs of four thousand or five thousand. Then, after the day's work was over, he would tell them the simple story of redemption. He had not yet learned the Telugu language sufficiently to make himself well understood in it, but he had done this: he had committed to memory John 3:16 in the Telugu tongue. And when, in talking to his people, he got 'stuck,' he would fall back on John 3:16. What a blessed thing to be able at least to repeat that! Then he would add other verses, day by day, to his little store of committed texts, until he had a sermon, about half-an-hour long, composed of a string of texts, like precious pearls. I have sometimes thought that I would rather have heard that than many modern sermons. So, once again the great text that God used for bringing souls to Christ was still Luther's little gospel: 'God so loved the world, that He gave His only begotten Son, that whosoever believeth in Him should not perish, but have everlasting life.'

THE FORTH PAIR OF WORDS - 'BELIEVE' AND 'HAVE'

Now we come to the fourth pair of words, 'believe,' and 'have.' You will see how important these words are. If God so loved, that He gave, what is necessary on the part of man? Only this, that he should *take* and *have*. That is very plain. If God loved you and the whole world, and gave you all that He had to give, all that remains for anybody to do is so to appreciate the love of God as to take the gift that God bestows, and so to have the gift that he takes. *Believing is receiving*. John, at the beginning of this gospel, tells us in what sense he is going to use the word 'believe.' That word occurs forty-four times in the gospel according to John, which is the great gospel of 'believing.' You do not find the word 'repent' in it once, but it is constantly repeating believing, believing, believing, and having life. In the twelfth and thirteenth verses of the first chapter, we read: 'To as many as *received* Him, to them gave He power to become the sons of God,' even to them that *believe on* His name.' 'To as many as *received*, even to those that *believed*.' That little word 'even' indicates that to *believe* is equivalent to *receive*. You may, in any one of those forty-four instances in this gospel, put the word 'receive' in the place of the word 'believe,' and still make good sense. For example: 'God so loved the world, that He gave His only begotten Son, that whosoever received Him might have everlasting life.'

You *have* what you *take*, do you not? It is a very simple thing to take what is given to you, and so to have it. That is, practically, *all there is in faith*. We may make faith obscure by talking too much about it, leading others to infer that there is in it some obscurity or mystery. Faith is very simple: it is taking the eternal life that is offered to you in Christ. If you can put forth your hand and receive a gift, you are able to put forth your will and receive the gift of God, even Jesus Christ, as your Saviour. I heard of an old lady, who was starting on a railway journey from an American station, out of which many trains move, although in different directions. Not having travelled much on the rail cars, she got confused. The old lady I speak of was going up to Bay City, Michigan, and she was afraid that she was, perhaps, on the wrong train. She reached over and showed her ticket to somebody in the seat immediately in front of her, and said, 'I want to go to Bay City. Is this the right train?' 'Yes madam.' Still, she was not quite at ease, for she thought that perhaps this fellow-passenger might have got into the wrong train too; so she stepped across the aisle of the car, and showed her ticket to another person, and was again told, 'Yes, madam, this is the right train.' But still the old lady was a little uncertain. In a few moments in came the conductor, or, as you call him, the guard; and she saw on his cap the conductor's ribbon, and she beckoned to him, and said, 'I want to go to Bay City; is this the right train?' 'Yes, madam, this is the right train.' And now she settled back in her seat, and was asleep before the train moved. That illustrates the simplicity of taking God at His Word. She did nothing but just receive the testimony of that conductor. That is all; but that is faith. The Lord Jesus Christ says to you, 'I love you; I died for you. Do you believe? Will you receive the salvation that I bought for you with My own blood?' You need do no work; not even so much as to get up and turn round. You need not go and ask your fellow-man across the church aisle, there, whether he has believed, and received, and been saved. All that you need to do is with all your heart to say, 'Dear Lord, I do take this salvation that Thou hast bought for me, and brought to me.' Simple, is it not? Yes, very simple: yet such receiving it is the soul of faith.

And what assurance but consciously *having* what you *take*? Somebody comes and offers me, tonight, some freewill offering. It costs me nothing. All that I have to do is to take what is given to me, and have it for my own. Faith is the *taking*, and the assurance is the conscious *having*; and that is all that I know about it.

THE FIFTH PAIR OF WORDS - 'PERISH' AND 'EVERLASTING LIFE'

There remains another pair of words. Would to God that I might impress the meaning of those terms, 'perish' and 'everlasting life'! What does 'perish' mean, and what does 'life' mean? When the prodigal son went into the far country, and had wasted his substance in riotous living, he came to himself; and he came back to his father, and he said, 'Father, I have sinned.' And the father said, 'This my son was dead, and is alive again. He was lost, and is found.' A son that is lost to his father is dead to his father, and a son that is found by his father is alive to his father. God said to Adam, 'In the day that thou eatest of the forbidden fruit, thou shalt surely die.' It did not mean that Adam should that day die, physically. It meant something worse than that. He *died to God* when he ate. One proof that he died to God when he ate the forbidden fruit is that, when the Lord came down to walk in the garden as the companion of Adam in the cool of the day, our first parents shrank from the presence of the Lord, and hid behind the trees of the garden, when they heard His footsteps and the sound of His voice. They were dead to sympathy towards God, dead to love towards God, dead to pleasure in God: and so they tried to get out of the way of God - as if it were possible to put a veil between them and Him. How do you know you are dead to

God? You want to get out of His way. You do not love the things that God loves; you would like to be independent of God's rule. You would like, if possible, to get into some corner of the universe where there is no God. You are like the men in America who went across to California, when the golden gates of that country were first opened, that they might enrich themselves. They tried to do without God, and there was a horrible state of sensuality and criminality there; and though there were, nominally, Christian families, and even Christian churches, these gold-seekers had left God on the other side of the Rocky Mountains, if not still further off, on the other side of the Alleghanies. They sought to get where there was no sanctuary, Bible, or family altar, and no restraint of Christian government, or recognition of a God above. The Psalmist twice says, 'The fool hath said in his heart, there is no God'; and if you leave out the italicised words, which are not in the original, it reads like this: 'The fool hath said in his heart, - No God!' That is, 'I wish that there were no God.' The impious man hates God. It is an uncomfortable thing for him to think that there is a Sovereign of all the earth who will judge all the works done in the body. It is uncomfortable to think that beyond the grave there lie the great assizes of the judgement day, and that one is unprepared to go into that judgement, and meet the judge. And so people try to make up their minds that there is no hereafter or judgement, and that there is no God. It is a sign that you are 'dead' when you would like that there should be no God, and you do not want God to have any rule over you. And what is the sign that you are alive? You come to yourself, and then you come to the Father? You would not have God out of the universe, if by the stroke of the hand, you could annihilate Him. You would not have the judgement-seat out of the universe, for that is the place where all wrongs are righted. You would not have heaven blotted out, for that is where,

> The quenched lamps of hope are all re-lighted,
> And the golden links of love are re-united;

and where there shall be no more sin, nor sorrow, nor sighing, nor tears; and where every shadow shall flee away. Paul says that the 'woman who lives in pleasure is dead while she liveth.' That is to say that, while she exists, she is so wrapped up in fashion, in ornaments, in the plaiting of the hair, and the putting on of gold and of gorgeous apparel - living for this world and her own indulgence, that she is dead to the things that are alone worth living for, and that take hold of the invisible, divine, and eternal.

Now, let us once more hear the word of the living God. God so loved you that He gave the best that He had to give, and all that He had to give; and while He gave to the whole world, He singled you out as the object of His love, and said, 'whosoever' - 'every creature.' And now that that gift is given to you, and there is no more to be given, God can do no more. He does not ask you to pay the one-thousandth part of a farthing for the priceless values represented in the Son of God. All that God can do now is to say to you that the very fact that you reject His dear Son is a proof that you are spiritually dead. Even though you dispute the fact, you are dead; as a deaf man may not understand how deaf he is, and the blind man may not understand the glories of sight, so a dead man cannot understand the energies of the living. And so the very fact that you think that you are not dead is another proof that you are. You have no sensibility even to the fact that you are spiritually without life. God comes, and says, 'Come back to Me, My prodigal and wandering son. You shall have the robe; you shall have the ring; you shall have the shoes. I will give them all to you with the absoluteness of an infinite love, and you shall take them, and have them because you take them.' Just the moment that you turn toward God, and say, 'My Father, I take the robe and the ring, and the shoes, and the place of a restored son in the Father's house,' you will live again; for you recognise your Father, and yourself as His son. You recognise His right to command, and your duty to obey. You recognise that the only place for a son is the home and the heart of his father. That is the proof that you are once more alive.

'Tell me how long it would take to change from death unto life?' Just as long, and no longer, as it takes you to turn round. Your back has been on God. You turn, and your face is toward Him. It will take no longer for a sinner to become a living son of God than that. Just put your heart into your acceptance of Jesus. Cast your whole will into the acceptance of the Fatherhood of God, renounce your sin and your rebellion, and take the salvation that is given to you freely as the sun gives its light, or the spring gives its stream; and before you turn round to go out of that church door, you may have this salvation, and perhaps enjoy in yourself the consciousness that you are saved!

BISHOP J. C. RYLE

John Charles Ryle was born in Cheshire in 1816, the son of a wealthy landowner and member of Parliament. He was educated at Eton and Oxford and it was intended that he should follow in his father's footsteps. But in 1838, during his final year at Oxford, Ryle was converted and in 1841 he entered the Christian ministry. He first ministered in Hampshire and then from 1844 to 1880 he ministered in country parishes in Suffolk, first at Helmingham then at Stradbroke. During this time he began to write, and although he published between 200 and 300 tracts which were translated into many languages and distributed all over the world, he was best known for his plain and lovely writings on practical and spiritual themes, particularly for his outstanding work, *Expository Thoughts on the Gospels*. His great aim in all his ministry, was to encourage strong and serious Christian living.

His writings and sermons are just as wise and relevant today as when he first put pen to paper and have been of great assistance to many ministers of the gospel down through the years and indeed a wonderful blessing to all who have read them.

The following sermon on John 3:16 was taken from his volume *The True Christian*.

7

SAVING FAITH

G od so loved the world, that He gave His only begotten Son, that whosoever believeth in Him should not perish, but have everlasting life. - John 3:16

In this verse, beloved, we have one of those 'heavenly things,' which our Lord had just spoken of to Nicodemus. Blessed indeed are the lips which spake it, and blessed are the hearts which can receive it! In this verse we find a treasury of the most precious truth, a mine of inexhaustible matter, a well of ever-flowing waters; and when we consider the simple words in which our Lord has here brought together the whole body of divinity, we must willingly confess, with those who heard Him preach, 'Never man spake like this man.' Listen, I pray you, once more - 'God so loved the world, that He gave His Only begotten Son, that whosoever believeth in Him should not perish, but have everlasting life.' There is hardly an expression that a child could not easily explain, and yet there are doctrines here which the wisest upon earth must humbly receive, if they would enter into the kingdom of heaven and sit down at the marriage supper of the Lamb. We learn in it, what the philosophers of old could never clear up - the history of God's dealing with mankind, and the terms which He offers for their acceptance. Here is life, and here is death; here you have the deserts of man, and here you have the free grace of God; here you see what all may expect who follow their own course, and here also the way, the truth, and the life is directly pointed out.

And at this particular season of the year, when we are about so soon to commemorate the mysterious birth of Him who in mercy to our sins consented to take our nature on Him and be born of a virgin, even Christ Jesus, we cannot, I think, do better than examine the things which are herein contained. May the Eternal Spirit, through whom He offered Himself, the great Teacher whom He promised to send, be amongst us: may He rouse the careless, fix the inattentive, and make the subject profitable to all.

Now I conceive the chief things to be noticed in this verse are:

1. The state of the world, that is, of all mankind.
2. The love of God.
3. The gift of His Son.
4. The means whereby we enjoy this gift.
5. And the promise attached to those who believe.

1. THE STATE OF THE WORLD, THAT IS, OF ALL MANKIND

First then, let us inquire what the Word of God has taught us respecting the world and the *world's character.* Now, the testimony of Scripture upon this head is so clear and explicit, that he who runs may read 'The whole world,' says John, 'lieth in wickedness.' Our first father, Adam, was indeed created in the image of God, pure and sinless; but in one day he fell from his high estate by eating the forbidden fruit, he broke God's express command and became at once a sinful creature; and now all we his children have by inheritance from him a wicked and a corrupt nature, a nature which clings to us from the moment of our birth, and which we show daily in our lives and conversation. In a word, we learn that from the hour of the fall our character has been established, that we are a sinful, a very sinful world.

Beloved, does this appear a hard saying? Do you think such a statement too strong? Away with the flattering thought! - We see it proved in Scripture, for every book of the Old Testament history tells the melancholy story of man's disobedience and man's unbelief in things pertaining to God. We read there of fearful judgements, such as the flood and the destruction of Sodom, yet men disregarded them, - of gracious mercies, such as the calling and protection of Israel, but men soon forgot them, - of inspired teachers and revelations from heaven, such as the law of Moses, and men did not obey them, - of special warnings, such as the voice of the prophets, and yet men did not believe them. Yes, beloved, we are a sinful world! Think not to say within yourselves, 'It may be so, but this happened in days of old; the world is better now.' It will not avail you. We have read it in Scripture, but we see it also around us, and you will find at this time, even under your own eyes, convincing proof that the charge is literally true. Let any, for instance, examine the columns of a county newspaper, and he will see there within a month enough to make his ears tingle. I speak as unto wise men, - judge ye what I say: will he not see accounts of nearly every sin which is abominable in the sight of God? Will he not read of anger, wrath, malice, blasphemy, theft, adultery, fornication, uncleanness, lasciviousness, emulations, variance, strife, seditions, envyings, murders, drunkenness, revellings, and such like: 'of the which,' says the apostle (Galatians 5:21), 'I tell you before, as I have also told you in time past, that they which do such things shall not inherit the kingdom of God.' And if such things take place in a land which is blessed with so much light and knowledge as our own, how much more should we find in countries where there is neither one nor the other! If men do these things in a green tree, oh, what shall they do in a dry?

Can you still doubt? I will go further. We see proof in ourselves. Let the best among you search his own heart; let him honestly cast up the number of evil thoughts and unholy ideas which pass through his imagination even in one single day - thoughts, I mean, which are known only to himself and the all-seeing God - and let him tell us whether it be not a most humiliating and soul-condemning calculation. Yes, dear friends, whether you will receive it or no, we are indeed a sinful world. It may be a humbling truth, but Scripture says it, and experience confirms it; and therefore we tell you that the world spoken of in our text is a world which lieth in wickedness, a corrupt world, a world which our great Maker and Preserver might have left to deserved destruction, and in so doing would have acted with perfect justice, because He has given us laws and they have been broken, promises and they have been despised, warnings and they have not been believed.

2.   THE LOVE OF GOD

Such is the world of which we form a part, and such is its character. And now let us hear what the feeling is with which God has been pleased to regard His guilty creatures. We were all under condemnation, without hope, without excuse; and what could stay the execution of the sentence? *It was the love of God.* 'God,' says our text, 'so loved the world.' He might have poured on us the vials of His wrath, as He did on the angels who kept not their first estate; but no! He spared us, 'God loved the world.' Justice demanded our punishment, holiness required we should be swept off the earth; but 'God loved the world.' Praised be His name, we had not to do with man's judgement, which may not show mercy, when a crime is proved; we were in the hands of One whose ways are not as our ways and whose thoughts are not as our thoughts, and hence, 'God so loved the world.' May we not well say with the apostle, 'O the depth of the riches both of the wisdom and knowledge of God!' (Romans 11:33). Consider, I pray you, this incomprehensible goodness! Do not many in this world think it no harm to remember injuries, and sometimes to resent them? Do we not find it hard to love those who have given us some slight offence? Or if we do profess to love them, do we make any endeavour to promote their happiness? Such, alas! is too seldom our practice; there is but little real affection in these hard hearts; but we are not dealt with according to our own ways, for the God of holiness has loved the sinful world, which has continually dishonoured and denied Him. Oh! Beloved, let us dwell much on such expressions as these, for they are more precious than rubies; let us bear them continually in mind, for they will not fail us in the day of trial, when temptation is strong and faith weak; let us write them on our hearts and in our memories, and we shall find them a strong consolation in the hour of death and on the bed of sickness. God is indeed love, and God loved the world.

3. THE GIFT OF HIS SON

Let us next inquire in what way it pleased God to manifest this love. We had all sinned. Who then could put away the sin and present us clean and spotless before His throne? We had all failed utterly of keeping His holy laws. Wherewithal then could we be clothed for the wedding-feast of our Master? Beloved, here is wisdom! This is the very point which the learned of this world could never understand. How, they have asked, can perfect justice and perfect mercy be reconciled? How can God justify His sinful creature, and yet be that Holy One whose law must needs be fulfilled? But all is explained in this simple verse, if ye can receive it; and thus it was - *'He gave His only begotten Son.'* Observe the magnitude of this gift - 'His only begotten Son.' Can anything give you a more tender idea of God's love? Observe again the expression 'He *gave*': not because we had merited anything, for it was a free gift; not for our deservings, for it was all of grace. 'By grace are ye saved,' says Paul to the Ephesians. 'The gift of God is eternal life,' says the same apostle to the Romans.

And for what purpose was His Son given? Beloved, He was given to atone for our guilt, by the sacrifice and death of Himself, as a lamb without spot and blemish; and by so doing He made a full, perfect, and sufficient oblation and satisfaction for the sins of the whole world. He was given to bear our iniquities and carry our transgressions upon the accursed tree, the cross; for being innocent Himself He was for our sakes accounted guilty, that we for His sake might be accounted pure. Nor is this all: He was given to fulfil the demands of that law which we have broken; and He did fulfil them. He 'was tempted in all points,' says Paul, 'like as we are, and yet without sin': the prince of this world had nothing in Him, and thus He brought in an everlasting righteousness, which like a pure white raiment is unto all and upon all them that believe (2 Corinthians 5:21).

4. THE MEANS WHEREBY WE ENJOY THIS GIFT

It would be easy to dwell upon this delightful branch of our subject, beloved, but we must pass on. How then are the benefits of this gift made our own? What are the means through which it is applied to our souls? What is the hand by which we lay hold on this remedy?

Here again our text supplies an answer. It is FAITH. Whosoever believeth (not with the head, remember: but with the heart), and believing comes to Christ with a confession of his own unrighteousness, and accepts Him as his only hope of salvation - is saved by Faith.

Consider now the beautiful simplicity of this way of life: we do not see written on the gate, Whosoever has prepared himself by long repentance - whosoever has begun to lead a new life - whosoever has done so many good works - whosoever has attended church so many times - whosoever has given so much in charity - these shall enter in here, and none else. No, dear friends; such announcements would frighten many a weary sinner, and these are fruits you will thankfully bring forth a hundredfold after you have entered: the only thing required of those who seek admission is faith, and he that approaches in simple childlike faith shall never be rejected. Hear how Paul speaks on this point (Romans 10:5-10). And, lest any one should suppose that God is a respecter of persons, that there is one way for the rich and another for the poor, one for the learned, another for the unlearned, he adds these comfortable words: 'For there is no difference between the Jew and the Greek: for the same Lord over all is rich unto all that call upon Him. For whosoever shall call upon the name of the Lord shall be saved.' But remember also - and I solemnly warn every one of this - there is no other way than the way of faith. God has not left each man to choose his own road to heaven, or his own path for coming unto Christ, but He has appointed one and no more, and no man shall enter into life except by this.

'If ye will not believe,' says Isaiah, 'surely ye shall not be established.' 'If ye believe not,' says our Lord, 'that I am He, ye shall die in your sins.' And hence we may learn this most important lesson, that although God so loved the world that He gave for it His only begotten Son, still the benefits of that gift can never be obtained by those who will not believe.

5.   THE PROMISE ATTACHED TO THOSE WHO BELIEVE

It remains for us in the last place to consider the *promises and consequences* which our text holds forth to the faithful. We read that 'whosoever believeth shall not perish, but have everlasting life.'

And is not this a promise the most acceptable to our nature that a gracious God could have devised? We know there is nothing the unconverted fear so much as death: people of the highest animal courage, who would shrink from no danger and encounter any difficulty, have been seen to tremble and turn pale at the approach of some pain or complaint which seems likely to bring their frail bodies to the grave. And why should this be so? - pain is not very bitter, and life with its cares and anxieties is not so very sweet as to account for it! No, beloved, the reason is this. Conscience tells every unconverted person, whether he likes to confess it or not, that after death shall come the judgement; conscience tells him that all shall be judged according to their works, - that he cannot abide this fiery trial, because he has sinned and not sought reconciliation, and he feels that he may one day have his part in the lake which burns with fire and brimstone. Hence it is that he thinks death a most unpleasant subject, and with all his pride of life stands in cowardly fear of his last day; and hence you may understand how blessed these words should be to a sinner's ear, that 'Whosoever believeth in Him shall not perish but have everlasting life.'

Observe now the contents of this promise; look narrowly into it, for it will stand a close examination. The believer shall not perish; this earthly tabernacle may indeed be dissolved, and laid in the grave and see corruption, but the true sting of that death is sin, and this his Saviour has taken on Him and put away. He shall not perish in the day of judgement; the second death can have no power over him; hell has no claims upon him, and then the words of our blessed Master shall be found a truth. 'This is the will of Him that sent Me, that every one which seeth the Son, and believeth on Him, may have everlasting life: and I will raise him up at the last day' (John 6:40). 'I am the resurrection and the life: he that believeth in Me, though he were dead, yet shall he live: And whosoever liveth and believeth in Me shall never die' (John 11:25,26).

And more than this: the believer shall have everlasting life. He shall be raised body and soul at our Lord's second coming. He shall have part in that first resurrection, which belongs only to the saints, and finally shall dwell for ever in that blessed place where 'there shall be no more death, neither sorrow, nor crying, neither shall there be any more pain: for the former things are passed away' (Revelation 21:4).

And now, beloved, judge yourselves whether it be not true, that our text contains a treasury of precious and most consoling doctrines, and he that can hear it without feeling its value may indeed tremble for the safety of his immortal soul. Believer, let it be thy care to carry home these comfortable words on which we have dwelt, and meditate upon them as thy daily food throughout the week which is now before thee. Let them be ever in thy mind, and prepare thee for that holy sacrament which Jesus has mercifully ordained; let them add strength to thy faith and growth to thy sanctification; let them increase thy humility and thy thankfulness, thy zeal for God's glory, and thy desire to show forth His praise, thy love towards Christ and thy love towards thy brethren; for surely, dear friends, if God so loved us, it is a small matter if we love our fellow-sinners.

And you too, dear brethren, who have dared hitherto, like Gallio, to care for none of these things, you also are appealed to in this text.

Learn then now, if you have not learned it yet, that this single verse, if there were no other, would be sufficient to condemn you in the last day, because it leaves you without excuse for remaining in your sins. You have deserved nothing but wrath; and yet behold, here is God willing to save, loving, giving, promising all things. Oh! Remember how great must be your guilt if you reject so great salvation. You are the very world that God has so loved; for your sakes He gave His only begotten Son, and even now, at this minute, He is inviting you, by me, His minister, to accept the mercy which He freely offers, to be reconciled with Him who will one day be the Judge of all (Isaiah 55:1,2; 1:18; Acts 16:31).

Come then, I entreat you, to your Father, in the name of Christ, for through Him we have boldness and access with confidence. Resist the attempts of the world, the flesh and the devil to detain you; resist even your best friend, if he would keep you back from God and tell you there will be a more convenient season than today. 'As though God did beseech you by us: we pray you in Christ's stead, be ye reconciled to God. For He hath made Him to be sin for us, who knew no sin; that we might be made the righteousness of God in Him' (2 Corinthians 5:20,21).

May God the Holy Ghost bless the words which we have spoken to the everlasting benefit of all your souls.

CHARLES HADDON SPURGEON

C harles Haddon Spurgeon is undoubtedly the most famous Baptist minister of the nineteenth century. Converted in 1850, he preached his first sermon at the age of sixteen. When he was eighteen he was invited to become the pastor of the Baptist congregation at Waterbeach, Cambridgeshire. Two years later, he was called to the New Park Street Church in London and within a year of his ministry the church was filled to overflowing. By the time he was twenty two years of age he was London's most popular preacher, and in order to facilitate the vast crowds who flocked to hear him preach, a much larger building, the Metropolitan Tabernacle, was built in 1861. It seated six thousand, and until his death in 1892, was consistently filled.

During the construction of the Tabernacle, Spurgeon preached to crowds of ten thousand in the Surrey Gardens Music Hall, and on one occasion, at the youthful age of twenty three, he preached to twenty four thousand in the Crystal Palace.

In 1855, he began to publish his sermons every Thursday, at the price of one penny, and today they make up the fifty seven volumes of *The Metropolitan Tabernacle Pulpit.*

This sermon was delivered by Spurgeon at the Metropolitan Tabernacle, on the evening of June 7th, 1885.

8

IMMEASURABLE LOVE

For God so loved the world, that He gave His only begotten Son, that whosoever believeth in Him should not perish, but have everlasting life. - John 3:16

I was very greatly surprised the other day, in looking over the list of texts from which I have preached, to find that I have no record of ever having spoken from this verse. This is all the more singular, because I can truly say that it might be put in the forefront of all my volumes of discourses as the sole topic of my life's ministry. It has been my one and only business to set forth the love of God to men in Christ Jesus. I heard lately of an aged minister of whom it was said, 'Whatever his text, he never failed to set forth God as love, and Christ as the atonement for sin.' I wish that much the same may be said of me. My heart's desire has been to sound forth as with a trumpet the good news that 'God so loved the world, that He gave His only begotten Son, that whosoever believeth in Him should not perish, but have everlasting life.'

We are about to meet around the communion table, and I cannot preach from this text anything but a simple gospel sermon. Can you desire a better preparation for communion? We have fellowship with

God and with one another upon the basis of the infinite love which is displayed in Jesus Christ our Lord. The gospel is the fair white linen cloth which covers the table on which the Communion Feast is set. The higher truths, those truths which belong to a more enlightened experience, those richer truths which tell of the fellowship of the higher life - all these are helpful to holy fellowship; but I am sure not more so than those elementary and foundation truths which were the means of our first entrance into the kingdom of God. Babes in Christ and men in Christ here feed upon one common food. Come, ye aged saints, be children again; and you that have long known your Lord, take up your first spelling-book, and go over your A B C again, by learning that God so loved the world, that He gave His Son to die, that man might live through him. I do not call you to an elementary lesson because you have forgotten your letters, but because it is a good thing to refresh the memory, and a blessed thing to feel young again. What the old folks used to call the Christ-cross Row contained nothing but the letters; and yet all the books in the language are made out of that line: therefore do I call you back to the cross, and to Him who bled thereon. It is a good thing for us all to return at times to our starting place, and make sure that we are in the way everlasting. The love of our espousals is most likely to continue if we again and again begin where God began with us, and where we first began with God. It is wise to come to Him afresh, as we came in that first day when, helpless, needy, heavy-laden, we stood weeping at the cross, and left our burden at the pierced feet. There we learned to look, and live, and love; and there would we repeat the lesson till we rehearse it perfectly in glory.

Tonight, we have to talk about the love of God: 'God so loved the world.' That love of God is a very wonderful thing, especially when we see it set upon a lost, ruined, guilty world. What was there in the world that God should love it? There was nothing lovable in it. No fragrant flower grew in that arid desert. Enmity to Him, hatred to His truth, disregard of His law, rebellion against His commandments; those were the thorns and briars which covered the waste land; but no desirable thing blossomed there. Yet, 'God loved the world,' says the text; 'so' loved it, that even the writer of the book of John could not tell us how much; but so greatly, so divinely, did He love it that He gave His Son, His only Son, to redeem the world from perishing, and to gather out of it a people to His praise.

Whence came that love? Not from anything outside of God Himself, God's love springs from Himself. He loves because it is His nature to do so. 'God is love.' As I have said already, nothing upon the face of the earth could have merited His love, though there was much to merit His displeasure. This stream of love flows from its own secret source in the eternal Deity, and it owes nothing to any earth-born rain or rivulet; it springs from beneath the everlasting throne, and fills itself full from the springs of the infinite. God loved because He would love. When we enquire why the Lord loved this man or that, we have to come back to our Saviour's answer to the question, 'Even so, Father, for so it seemed good in Thy sight.' God has such love in His nature that He must needs let it flow forth to a world perishing by its own wilful sin; and when it flowed forth it was so deep, so wide, so strong, that even inspiration could not compute its measure, and therefore the Holy Spirit gave us that great little word SO, and left us to attempt the measurement, according as we perceive more and more of love divine.

Now, there happened to be an occasion upon which the great God could display His immeasurable love, The world had sadly gone astray; the world had lost itself; the world was tried and condemned; the world was given over to perish, because of its offences; and there was need for help. The fall of Adam and the destruction of mankind made ample room and verge enough for love almighty. Amid the ruins of humanity there was space for showing how much Jehovah loved the sons of men; for the compass of His love was no less than the world, the object of it no less than to deliver men from going down to the pit, and the result of it no less than the finding of a ransom for them. The far-reaching purpose of that love was both negative and positive; that believing in Jesus, men might not perish, but have eternal life. The desperate disease of man gave occasion for the introduction of that divine remedy which God alone could have devised and supplied. By the plan of mercy, and the great gift which was needed for carrying it out, the Lord found means to display His boundless love to guilty men. Had there been no fall, and no perishing, God might have shown His love to us as He does to the pure and perfect spirits that surround His throne; but He never could have commended His love to us to such an extent as He now does. In the gift of His only begotten Son, God commended His love to us, in that while we were yet sinners in due time Christ died for the ungodly. The black background of sin makes the bright line of love shine out the more clearly. When the lightning writes the name of the Lord with flaming finger across the black brow of the tempest, we are compelled to see it; so when love inscribes the cross upon the jet tablet of our sin, even blind eyes must see that 'herein is love.'

I might handle my text in a thousand different ways tonight; but for simplicity's sake, and to keep to the one point of setting forth the love of God, I want to make you see how great that love is by five different particulars.

1. THE GIFT

The first is the GIFT: 'God so loved the world, that *He gave His only begotten Son.*' Men who love much will give much, and you may usually measure the truth of love by its self-denials and sacrifices. That love which spares nothing, but spends itself to help and bless its object, is love indeed, and not the mere name of it. Little love forgets to bring water for the feet, but great love breaks its box of alabaster and lavishes its precious ointment.

Consider, then, *what this gift was* that God gave. I should have to labour for expression if I were to attempt to set forth to the full this priceless boon; and I will not court a failure by attempting the impossible. I will only invite you to think of the sacred Person whom the Great Father gave in order that He might prove His love to men. It was His only begotten Son - His beloved Son, in who He was well pleased. None of us had ever such a Son to give. Ours are the sons of men; His was the Son of God. The Father gave His other Self, one with Himself. When the great God gave His Son He gave God Himself for Jesus is not in His eternal nature less than God. When God gave God for us He gave Himself. What more could He give? God gave His all: He gave Himself. Who can measure this love?

Judge, ye fathers, how ye love your sons: could ye give them to die for your enemy? Judge, ye that have an only son, how your hearts are entwined about your first-born, your only begotten. There was no higher proof of Abraham's love to God than when he did not withhold from God his son, his only son, his Isaac whom he loved; and there can certainly be no greater display of love than for the Eternal Father to give His only begotten Son to die for us. No living thing will readily lose its offspring; man has peculiar grief when his son is taken; has not God more? A story has often been told of the fondness of parents for their children; how in a famine in the East a father and mother were reduced to absolute starvation, and the only possibility of preserving the life of the family was to sell one of the children into slavery. So they considered it. The pinch of hunger became unbearable, and their children pleading for bread tugged so painfully at their heart-strings, that they must entertain the idea of selling one to save the lives of the rest. They had four sons. Who of these should be sold? It must not be the first: how could they spare their first-born? The second was so strangely like his father that he seemed a reproduction of him, and the mother said that she would never part with him. The third was so singularly like the mother that the father said he would sooner die than that this dear boy should go into bondage; and as for the fourth, he was their Benjamin, their last, their darling, and they could not part with him. They concluded that it were better for them all to die together than willingly to part with any one of their children. Do you not sympathise with them? I see you do. Yet God so loved us that, to put it very strongly, He seemed to love us better than His only Son, and did not spare Him that He might spare us. He permitted His Son to perish from among men 'that whosoever believeth in Him might not perish, but have everlasting life.'

If you desire to see the love of God in this great procedure you must consider *how He gave His Son.* He did not give His Son, as you might do, to some profession in the pursuit of which you might still enjoy his company; but He gave His Son to exile among men. He sent Him down to yonder manger, united with a perfect manhood, which at the first was in an infant's form. There He slept, where horned oxen fed! The Lord God sent the heir of all things to toil in a carpenter's shop; to drive the nail, and push the plane, and use the saw. He sent Him down amongst scribes and Pharisees, whose cunning eyes watched Him, and whose cruel tongues scourged Him with base slanders. He sent Him down to hunger, and thirst, amid poverty so dire that He had not where to lay His head. He sent Him down to the scourging and the crowning with thorns, to the giving of His back to the smiters and His cheeks to those that plucked off the hair. At length He gave Him up to death - a felon's death, the death of the crucified. Behold that cross and see the anguish of Him that dies upon it, and mark how the Father has so given Him, that He hides His face from Him, and seems as if He would not own Him! 'Lama sabachthani' tells us how fully God gave His Son to ransom the souls of the sinful. He gave Him to be made a curse for us; He gave Him that He might die 'the just for the unjust, to bring us to God.'

Dear sirs, I can understand your giving up your children to go to India on Her Majesty's service, or to go out to the Cameroons or the Congo upon the errands of our Lord Jesus. I can well comprehend your yielding them up even with the fear of a pestilential climate before you, for if they die they will die honourably in a glorious cause; but could you think of parting with them to die a felon's death, upon a gibbet, execrated by those whom they sought to bless, stripped naked in body and deserted in mind? Would not that be too much? Would you not cry, 'I cannot part with my son for such wretches as these. Why should he be put to a cruel death for such abominable beings, who even wash their hands in the blood of their best friend'? Remember that our Lord Jesus died what His countrymen considered to be an accursed death. To the Romans it was the death of a condemned slave, a death which had all the elements of pain, disgrace, and scorn mingled in it to the uttermost. 'But God commendeth His love toward us, in that, while we were yet sinners, Christ died for us.' Oh, wondrous stretch of love, that Jesus Christ should die!

Yet, I cannot leave this point till I have you notice *when God gave His Son*, for there is love in the time. 'God so loved the world that He gave His only begotten Son.' But when did He do that? In His eternal purpose He did this from before the foundation of the world. The words here used, 'He gave His only begotten Son,' cannot relate exclusively to the death of Christ, for Christ was not dead at the time of the utterance of this third chapter of John. Our Lord had just been speaking with Nicodemus, and that conversation took place at the beginning of His ministry. The fact is that Jesus was always the gift of God. The promise of Jesus was made in the garden of Eden almost as soon as Adam fell. On the spot where our ruin was accomplished, a Deliverer was bestowed Whose heel should be bruised, but Who should break the serpent's head beneath His foot.

Throughout the ages the great Father stood to His gift. He looked upon His only begotten Son as man's hope, the inheritance of the chosen seed, who in Him would possess all things. Every sacrifice was God's renewal of His gift of grace, a reassurance that He had bestowed the gift, and would never draw back therefrom. The whole system of types under the law betokened that in the fullness of time the Lord would in very deed give up His Son, to be born of a woman, to bear the iniquities of His people, and to die the death on their behalf. I greatly admire this pertinacity of love; for many a man in a moment of generous excitement can perform a supreme act of benevolence, and yet could not bear to look at it calmly, and consider it from year to year; the slow fire of anticipation would have been unbearable. If the Lord should take away yonder dear boy from his mother, she would bear the blow with some measure of patience, heavy as it would be to her tender heart; but suppose that she were credibly informed that on such a day her boy must die, and thus had from year to year to look upon him as one dead, would it not cast a cloud over every hour of her future life? Suppose also that she knew he would be hanged upon a tree to die, as one condemned; would it not embitter her existence? If she could withdraw from such a trial, would she not? Assuredly she would. Yet the Lord God spared not His own Son, but freely delivered Him up for us all, doing it in His heart from age to age. Herein is love: love which many waters could not quench: love eternal, inconceivable, infinite!

Now, as this gift refers not only to our Lord's death but to the ages before it, so it includes all the ages afterwards. God 'so loved the world that He gave' - and still gives - 'His only begotten Son, that whosoever believeth in Him might not perish, but have everlasting life.' The Lord is giving Christ away tonight. Oh, that thousands of you may gladly accept the gift unspeakable! Will anyone refuse? This good gift, this perfect gift, - can you decline it? Oh, that you may have faith to lay hold on Jesus, for thus He will be yours. He is God's free gift to all free receivers; a full Christ for empty sinners. If you can but hold out your empty willing hand, the Lord will give Christ to you at this moment. Nothing is freer than a gift. Nothing is more worth having than a gift which comes fresh from the hand of God, as full of effectual power as ever it was. The fountain is eternal, but the stream from it is as fresh as when first the fountain was opened. There is no exhausting this gift.

'Dear dying Lamb, Thy precious blood
Shall never lose its power
Till all the ransomed church of God
Be saved to sin no more.'

See, then, what is the love of God, that He gave His Son from of old, and has never revoked the gift. He stands to His gift, and continues still to give His dear Son to all who are willing to accept Him. Out of the riches of His grace He has given, is giving, and will give the Lord Jesus Christ, and all the priceless gifts which are contained in Him, to all needy sinners who will simply trust Him.

I call upon you from this first point to admire the love of God, because of the transcendent greatness of His gift to the world, even the gift of His only begotten Son.

2.   THE PLAN OF SALVATION

Now notice secondly, and, I think I may say, with equal admiration, the love of God in THE PLAN OF SALVATION. He has put it thus: 'that whosoever believeth in Him should not perish, but have everlasting life.' The way of salvation is extremely simple to understand, and exceedingly easy to practise, when once the heart is made willing and obedient. The method of the covenant of grace differs as much from that of the covenant of works as light from darkness. It is not said that God has given His Son to all who will keep His law, for that we could not do, and therefore the gift would have been available to none of us. Nor is it said that He has given His Son to all that experience terrible despair and bitter remorse, for that is not felt by many who nevertheless are the Lord's own people. But the great God has given His own Son, that 'whosoever believeth in Him' should not perish. Faith, however slender, saves the soul. Trust in Christ is the certain way of eternal happiness.

Now, what is it to believe in Jesus? It is just this: it is to trust yourself with Him. If your hearts are ready, though you have never believed in Jesus before, I trust you will believe in Him now. O Holy Spirit graciously make it so.

What is it to believe in Jesus?

It is, first, to give your *firm and cordial assent* to the truth, that God did send His Son, born of a woman, to stand in the room and stead of guilty men, and that God did cause to meet on Him the iniquities of us all, so that He bore the punishment due to our transgressions, being made a curse for us. We must heartily believe the Scripture which saith, - 'the chastisement of our peace was upon Him; and with His stripes we are healed.' I ask for your assent to the grand doctrine of substitution, which is the marrow of the gospel. Oh, may God the Holy Spirit lead you to give a cordial assent to it at once; for wonderful as it is, it is a fact that God was in Christ reconciling the world unto Himself, not imputing their trespasses unto them. Oh that you may rejoice that this is true, and be thankful that such a blessed fact is revealed by God Himself. Believe that the substitution of the Son of God is certain; cavil not at the plan, nor question its validity, or efficacy, as many do. Alas! they kick at God's great sacrifice, and count it a sorry invention. As for me, since God has ordained to save man by a substitutionary sacrifice, I joyfully agree to His method, and see no reason to do anything else but admire it and adore the Author of it. I joy and rejoice that such a plan should have been thought of, whereby the justice of God is vindicated, and His mercy is set free to do all that He desires. Sin is punished in the person of the Christ, yet mercy is extended to the guilty. In Christ mercy is sustained by justice, and justice is satisfied by an act of mercy. The worldly wise say hard things about this device of infinite wisdom; but as for me, I love the very name of the cross, and count it to be the centre of wisdom, the focus of love, the heart of righteousness. This is a main point of faith - to give a hearty assent to the giving of Jesus to suffer in our place and stead, to agree with all our soul and mind to this way of salvation.

The second thing is that you do *accept this for yourself*. In Adam's sin, you did not sin personally, for you were not then in existence; yet you fell; neither can you now complain thereof, for you have willingly endorsed and adopted Adam's sin by committing personal transgressions. You have laid your hand, as it were, upon Adam's sin, and made it your own, by committing personal and actual sin. Thus you perished by the sin of another, which you adopted and endorsed; and in like manner must you be saved by the righteousness of another, which you are to accept and appropriate. Jesus has offered an atonement, and that atonement becomes yours when you accept it by putting your trust in Him. I want you now to say,

> 'My faith doth lay her hand
> On that dear head of Thine,
> While, like a penitent, I stand,
> And here confess my sin.'

Surely this is no very difficult matter. To say that Christ Who hung upon the cross shall be my Christ, my surety, needs neither stretch of intellect, nor splendour of character; and yet it is the act which brings salvation to the soul.

One thing more is needful; and that is *personal trust*. First comes assent to the truth, then acceptance of that truth for yourself, and then a simple trusting of yourself wholly to Christ, as a substitute. The essence of faith is trust, reliance, dependence. Fling away every other confidence of every sort, save confidence in Jesus. Do not allow a ghost of a shade of a shadow of a confidence in anything that you can do, or in anything that you can be; but look alone to Him whom God has set forth to be the propitiation for sin. This I do at this very moment; will you not do the same? Oh, may the sweet Spirit of God lead you now to trust in Jesus!

See, then, the love of God in putting it in so plain, so easy a way. Oh, thou broken, crushed and despairing sinner, thou canst not work, but canst thou not believe that which is true? Thou canst not sigh; thou canst not cry; thou canst not melt thy stony heart; but canst thou not believe that Jesus died for thee, and that He can change that heart of thine and make thee a new creature? If thou canst believe this, then trust in Jesus to do so, and thou art saved; for he that believeth in Him is justified. 'He that believeth in Him *hath* everlasting life.' He is a saved man. His sins are forgiven him. Let him go his way in peace and sin no more.

I admire, first, the love of God in the great gift, and then in the great plan by which that gift becomes available to guilty men.

3. THE PERSONS FOR WHOM THIS PLAN IS AVAILABLE

Thirdly, the love of God shines forth with transcendent brightness in a third point, namely, in THE PERSONS FOR WHOM THIS PLAN IS AVAILABLE, and for whom this gift is given. They are described in these words - 'Whosoever believeth in Him.' There is in the text a word which has no limit - 'God so loved the world'; but then comes in the descriptive limit, which I beg you to notice with care: 'He gave His only begotten Son *that whosoever believeth in Him* might not perish.' God did not so love the world that any man who does not believe in Christ shall be saved; neither did God so give His Son that any man shall be saved who refuses to believe in Him. See how it is put - 'God so loved the world, that He gave His only begotten Son, that whosoever believeth in Him should not perish.' Here is the compass of the love: while every unbeliever is excluded, every believer is included. 'Whosoever believeth in Him.' Suppose there be a man who has been guilty of all the lusts of the flesh to an infamous degree, suppose that he is so detestable that he is only fit to be treated like a moral leper, and shut up in a separate house for fear he should contaminate those who hear or see him; yet if that man shall believe in Jesus Christ, he shall at once be made clean from his defilement, and shall not perish because of his sin. And suppose there be another man who, in the pursuit of his selfish motives, has ground down the poor, has robbed his fellow-traders, and has even gone so far as to commit actual crime of which the law has taken cognisance, yet if he believes in the Lord Jesus Christ he shall be led to make restitution, and his sins shall be forgiven him. I once heard of a preacher addressing a company of men in chains, condemned to die for murder and other crimes. They were such a drove of beasts to all outward appearances that it seemed hopeless to preach to them; yet were I set to be chaplain to such a wretched company I should not hesitate to tell them that 'God so loved the world, that He gave His only begotten Son, that *whosoever* believeth in Him should not perish, but have everlasting life.' O man, if thou wilt believe in Jesus as the Christ, however horrible thy past sins have been they shall be blotted out; thou shalt be saved from the power of thine evil habits; and thou shalt begin again like a child newborn, with a new and true life, which God shalt give thee. 'Whosoever believeth in Him,' - that takes you in, my aged friend, now lingering within a few tottering steps of the grave. O grey-headed sinner, if you believe in Him, you shall not perish. The text also includes you, dear boy, who have scarcely entered your teens as yet: if you believe in Him, you shall not perish. That takes you in, fair maiden, and gives you hope and joy while yet young. That comprehends all of us, provided we believe in the Lord Jesus Christ. Neither can all the devils in hell find out any reason why the man that believes in Christ shall be lost, for it is written, 'Him that cometh to Me I will in no wise cast out.' Do they say, 'Lord, he has been so long in coming'? The Lord replies, - 'Has he come? Then I will not cast Him out for all his delays.' But, Lord, he went back after making a profession. 'Has he at length come? Then I will not cast him out for all his backslidings.' But, Lord, he was a foul-mouthed blasphemer. 'Has he come to Me? Then I will not cast him out for all his blasphemies.' But, says one, 'I take exception to the salvation of this wicked wretch. He has behaved so abominably that in all justice he ought to be sent to hell.' Just so. But if he repents of his sin and believes in the Lord Jesus Christ, whoever he may be, he shall not be sent there. He shall be changed in character, so that he shall never perish, but have eternal life.

Now, observe, that this 'whosoever' makes a grand sweep; for it encircles all degrees of faith. 'Whosoever believeth in Him.' It may be that he has no full assurance; it may be that he has no assurance at all; but if he has faith, true and childlike, by it he shall be saved. Though his faith be so little that I must needs put on my spectacles to see it, yet Christ will see it and reward it. His faith is such a tiny grain of mustard seed that I look and look again but hardly discern it, and yet it brings him eternal life, and it is itself a living thing. The Lord can see within that mustard seed a tree among whose branches the birds of the air shall make their nests.

'My faith is feeble, I confess,
I faintly trust Thy Word;
But wilt Thou pity me the less?
Be that far from Thee, Lord!'

O Lord Jesus if I cannot take Thee up in my arms as Simeon did, I will at least touch Thy garment's hem as the poor diseased woman did to whom Thy healing virtue flowed. It is written, 'God so loved the world, that He gave His only begotten Son, that whosoever believeth in Him should not perish, but have everlasting life.' That means me. I cannot preach at length to you tonight; but I would preach with strength. Oh that this truth may soak into your souls. Oh you that feel yourselves guilty; and you that feel guilty because you do not feel guilty; you that are broken in heart because your heart will not break; you that feel that you cannot feel; it is to you that I would preach salvation in Christ by faith. You groan because you cannot groan; but whoever you may be, you are still within the range of this mighty word, that 'whosoever believeth in Him should not perish, but have eternal life.'

Thus have I commended God's love to you in those three points - the divine gift, the divine method of saving, and the divine choice of the persons to whom salvation comes.

4.   THE DELIVERANCE

Now fourthly, another beam of divine love is to be seen in the negative blessing here stated, namely, in THE DELIVERANCE implied in the words, 'that whosoever believeth in Him should *not perish.*'

I understand that word to mean that whosoever believes in the Lord Jesus Christ shall not perish, though he is ready to perish. His sins would cause him to perish, but he shall never perish. At first he has a little hope in Christ, but its existence is feeble. It will soon die out, will it not? No, his faith shall not perish, for this promise covers it - 'Whosoever believeth in Him shall not perish.' The penitent has believed in Jesus, and therefore he has begun to be a Christian; 'Oh,' cries an enemy, 'let him alone: he will soon be back among us; he will soon be as careless as ever.' Listen. 'Whosoever believeth in Him shall not perish,' and therefore he will not return to his former state. This proves the final perseverance of the saints; for if the believer ceased to be a believer he would perish; and as he cannot perish, it is clear that he will continue a believer. If thou believest in Jesus, thou shalt never leave off believing in Him; for that would be to perish. If thou believest in Him, thou shalt never delight in thine old sins; for that would be to perish. If thou believest in Him, thou shalt never lose spiritual life. How canst thou lose that which is everlasting? If thou wert to lose it, it would prove that it was not everlasting, and thou wouldst perish; and thus thou wouldst make this word to be of no effect. Whosoever with his heart believeth in Christ is a saved man, not for tonight only, but for all the nights that ever shall be, and for that dread night of death, and for that solemn eternity which draws so near. 'Whosoever believeth in Him shall not perish;' but he shall have a life that cannot die, a justification that cannot be disputed, an acceptance which shall never cease.

What is it to perish? It is to lose all hope in Christ, all trust in God, all light in life, all peace in death, all joy, all bliss, all union with God. This shall never happen to thee if thou believest in Christ. If thou believest, thou shalt be chastened when thou dost wrong, for every child of God comes under discipline; and what son is there whom the Father chasteneth not? If thou believest, thou mayest doubt and fear as to thy state, as a man on board a ship may be tossed about; but thou hast gotten on board a ship that never can be wrecked. He that hath union with Christ has union with perfection, omnipotence and glory. He that believeth is a member of Christ: will Christ lose His members? How should Christ be perfect if He lost even His little finger? Are Christ's members to rot off, or to be cut off? Impossible. If thou hast faith in Christ thou art a partaker of Christ's life, and thou canst not perish. If men were trying to drown me, they could not drown my foot as long as I had my head above the water; and as long as our Head is above water, up yonder in the eternal sunshine, the least limb of His body can never be destroyed. He that believeth in Jesus is united to Him, and He must live because Jesus lives. Oh what a word is this, 'I give unto My sheep eternal life, and they shall never perish, neither shall any man pluck them out of My hand. My Father which gave them Me is greater than all; and no man is able to pluck them out of My Father's hand.' I feel that I have a grand gospel to preach to you when I read that whosoever believeth in Jesus shall not perish. I would not give two pins for that trumpery, temporary salvation which some proclaim, which floats to the soul for a time and then ebbs away to apostasy. I do not believe that the man who is once in Christ may live in sin and delight in it, and yet be saved. That is abominable teaching, and none of mine. But I believe that the man who is in Christ will *not* live in sin, for he is saved from it; nor will he return to his old sins and abide in them, for the grace of God will continue to save him from his sins. Such a change is wrought by regeneration that the newborn man cannot abide in sin, nor find comfort in it, but he loves holiness and makes progress in it. The Ethiopian may change his skin, and the leopard his spots, but only grace divine can work the change; and when divine grace has done the deed the blackamore will remain white, and the leopard's spots will never return. It would be as great a miracle to undo the work of God as to do it; and to destroy the new creation would require as great a power as to make it. As only God can create, so only God can destroy; and He will never destroy the work of His own hands. Will God begin to build and not finish? Will He commence a warfare and end it before He has won the victory? What would the devil say if Christ were to begin to save a soul and fail in the attempt? If there should come to be souls in hell that were believers in Christ, and yet did perish, it would cast a cloud upon the diadem of our exalted Lord. It cannot, shall not, be. Such is the love of God, that whosoever believeth in His dear Son shall not perish: in this assurance we greatly rejoice.

5.   IN THE POSSESSION

The last commendation of His love lies in *the positive* - IN THE POSSESSION. I shall have to go in a measure over the same ground again. Let me therefore be the shorter. God gives to every man that believes in Christ everlasting life. The moment thou believest there trembles into thy bosom a vital spark of heavenly flame which never shall be quenched. In that same moment when thou dost cast thyself on Christ, Christ comes to thee in the living and incorruptible word which liveth and abideth for ever. Though there should drop into thy heart but one drop of the heavenly water of life, remember this, - he hath said it who cannot lie, - 'The water that I shall give him shall be in him a well of water springing up into everlasting life.' When I first received everlasting life I had no idea what a treasure had come to me. I knew that I had obtained something very extraordinary, but of its superlative value I was not aware. I did but look to Christ in the little chapel, and I received eternal life. I looked to Jesus and He looked on me; and we were one for ever. That moment my joy surpassed all bounds, just as my sorrow had aforetime driven me to an extreme of grief. I was perfectly at rest in Christ, satisfied with Him, and my heart was glad; but I did not know that this grace was everlasting life till I began to read in the Scriptures, and to know more fully the value of the jewel which God had given me. The next Sunday I went to the same chapel, as it was very natural that I should. But I never went afterwards, for this reason, that during my first week in the new life that was in me had been compelled to fight for its existence, and a conflict with the old nature had been vigorously carried on. This I knew to be a special token of the indwelling of grace in my soul; but in that same chapel I heard a sermon upon, 'O wretched man that I am! who shall deliver me from the body of this death?' And the preacher declared that Paul was not a Christian when he had that experience. Babe as I was, I knew better than to believe so absurd a statement. What but divine grace could produce such a sighing and crying after deliverance from indwelling sin? I felt that a person who could talk such nonsense knew little of the life of a true believer. I said to myself, 'What! am I not alive because I feel a conflict within me? I never felt this fight when I was an unbeliever. When I was not a Christian I never groaned to be set free from sin. This conflict is one of the surest evidences of my new birth, and yet this man cannot see it; he may be a good exhorter to sinners, but he cannot feed believers.' I resolved to go into that pasture no more, for I could not feed therein. I find that the struggle becomes more and more intense; each victory over sin reveals another army of evil tendencies, and I am never able to sheathe my sword, nor cease from prayer and watchfulness.

I cannot advance an inch without praying my way, nor keep the inch I gain without watching and standing fast. Grace alone can preserve and perfect me. The old nature will kill the new nature if it can; and to this moment the only reason why my new nature is not dead is this - because it cannot die. If it could have died, it would have been slain long ago; but Jesus said, 'I give unto My sheep eternal life'; 'he that believeth on Me hath everlasting life'; and therefore the believer cannot die. The only religion which will save you is one that you cannot leave, because it possesses you, and will not leave you. If you hold a doctrine which you can give up, give it up; but if the doctrines are burnt into you so that as long as you live you must hold them, and so that if you were burnt every ash would hold that same truth in it, because you are impregnated with it, then you have found the right thing. You are not a saved man unless Christ has saved you for ever. But that which has such a grip of you that its grasp is felt in the core of your being is the power of God. To have Christ living in you, and the truth ingrained in your very nature - O sirs, *this* is the thing that saves the soul, and nothing short of it. It is written in the text, 'God so loved the world that He gave His only begotten Son, that whosoever believeth in Him should not perish, but have everlasting life.' What is this but a life that shall last through your three-score years and ten; a life that shall last you should you outlive a century; a life that will still flourish when you lie at the grave's mouth; a life that will abide when you have quitted the body, and left it rotting in the tomb; a life that will continue when your body is raised again, and you shall stand before the judgement-seat of Christ; a life that will outshine those stars and yon sun and moon; a life that shall be co-eval with the life of the Eternal Father? As long as there is a God, the believer shall not only exist, but live. As long as there is a heaven, you shall enjoy it; as long as there is a Christ, you shall live in His love; and as long as there is an eternity, you shall continue to fill it with delight.

God bless you and help you to believe in Jesus - Amen.

DR. R. A. TORREY

D r. Reuben Archer Torrey grew up in a wealthy home, and was educated at Yale University and Divinity School. It was while he was studying at Yale that his life took a downward turn and he became an agnostic and also a heavy drinker. But looking back on those days he would say that he had a conviction in his heart that some day he was going to be a preacher of the Gospel, and indeed the Lord did save him while he was in his senior year in college.

When at Yale Divinity School he was largely influenced by D. L. Moody, who had come to town for a Gospel Campaign. Recognising his outstanding scholastic abilities and his evangelistic zeal, Moody later hand picked him to become superintendent of Moody Bible Institute, and soon he became his right hand man.

He was pastor of Moody Church from 1894 - 1906, and in 1912, he became dean of BIOLA, where he served until 1924.

After Moody's death he left the Bible Institute to carry on the great soul winning campaigns of the Moody pattern in Australia, New Zealand, England and America.

When he died in 1928 he had written more than forty books. This sermon is taken from his book *Real Salvation.*

9

HOW GOD LOVED
THE WORLD

F or God so loved the world, that He gave His only begotten
Son, that whosoever believeth in Him should not perish, but
have everlasting life.' - John 3:16

God has given me for my text tonight that verse of Scripture
which I suppose has been used to the salvation of more people than
any other verse in the Bible. It is John 3:16: 'God so loved the world,
that He gave His only begotten Son, that whosoever believeth in
Him should not perish, but have everlasting life.' Thousands of people
have been saved by that wonderful verse; tens of thousands, hundreds
of thousands, by simply reading it in the Bible, by simply seeing it
painted on the wall, by simply having it presented to them on a piece
of cardboard. If there were time I could tell you tonight of a boy
who began to read the Bible through, and was brought under very
deep conviction of sin by just reading the Bible. As he read on and
on, he came to the New Testament and to the Gospel of John, and to
the third chapter and the sixteenth verse, and there he read, 'God so
loved the world, that He gave His only begotten Son, that whosoever

believeth in Him should not perish, but have everlasting life.' And the moment he saw it, he saw Christ on the cross for his sins, his burden all rolled away, and he found peace. I hope that hundreds tonight will be converted in this hall through my text, whether you hear my sermon or not. This text tells us some very important things about the love of God. It tells us that our salvation begins in God's love. We are not saved because we love God; we are saved because God loves us. Our salvation begins in God's loving us, and it ends in our loving God.

THE LOVE OF GOD IS UNIVERSAL

The first thing our text teaches us about the love of God is that THE LOVE OF GOD IS UNIVERSAL. 'God so loved the world' - not some part of it, not some elect people, not some select class - 'but God so loved the world.' God loves the rich, but God loves the poor just as much as He loves the rich. If there should come into Bingley Hall tonight one of the wealthiest men or women in Birmingham, and if when I give out the invitation they should stand up and accept Christ, a great many of you people would be greatly pleased. So would I, for the rich need to hear the Gospel just as much as the poor, and they are not nearly so likely to. But if some poor man should come in here tonight, some man that has not a penny, some man that does not even know where he is going to sleep tonight, and if that man should stand up and take Christ, a good many of you people would not think it amounted to much, but God would be just as pleased to see the poorest man or woman in this building accept Christ, as He would be to see the richest millionaire that you have in Birmingham. God loves the educated, but God loves the uneducated just as much. God loves the great scholar, the man of science, the university professor, and the student, but God loves the man who can't read or write just as much as He loves the most brilliant scientist or philosopher that there is on earth. If some of your university professors should come in here tonight, and should be converted, some of you people would be delighted. You would go out saying, 'Oh, a wonderful thing happened in Bingley Hall. One of our learned professors came up there and was converted.' But if some man or woman here tonight that can't even read or write should stand up and accept Christ, some of you people would not think it amounted to much, but God would be just as much pleased as He would over the conversion of that university professor. But the most wonderful thing of all about it is this - that God loves the moral, the upright, the virtuous, the righteous, and God just as truly loves the sinner, the outcast, the abandoned, the profligate, the bad as He does the good.

One night I was visiting one of the members of my church, and his little girl was playing around the room. The child did something naughty - I have forgotten what it was - and her father called out, 'Don't be naughty. If you are a good girl God will love you, but if you are not, God won't love you.' I said, 'Charlie, what nonsense are you teaching that child of yours? That is not what my Bible teaches. My Bible teaches that God loves the sinner just as truly as He loves the saint.' And do you know, friends, it is so hard to make people believe this, that God does love the sinner, that God does love the outcast, that this is the truth that the Bible emphasises the most. For example, turn in your Bible to Romans 5:8: 'God commendeth His love toward us, in that while we were yet sinners, Christ died for us.'

I was preaching one night in the city of Minneapolis in America - a hot summer's night, so hot that the window frames were all out at the back to let a little fresh air in, and the room was packed. Away down at the back end of the room a man was sitting where the window frame had been taken out, and when I gave out the invitation for all who wished to be saved that night to hold up their hands, that man sitting in the window raised his hand. But as soon as I pronounced the benediction that man started out for the door. I forgot all about my after-meeting. I don't know to this day what became of that after-meeting. All I saw was that man starting for the door, and I started after him. I caught him just as he turned to descend the stairway. I laid my hand upon his shoulder just as he turned the corner. I said to him, 'My friend, you held up your hand to say you wanted to be saved.' 'Yes, I did.' 'Why didn't you stay, then, to the second meeting?' He said, 'It is no use.' 'Why?' I said; 'God loves you.' He said, 'You don't know who you are talking to.' I said, 'I don't care who I am talking to. I know God loves you.' He said, 'I am the meanest thief in Minneapolis.' 'Well,' I said, 'if you are the meanest thief in Minneapolis I can prove to you from the Bible that God loves you.' I opened my Bible to Romans 5:8, and I read, 'God commendeth His love toward us, in that while we were yet sinners, Christ died for us.' 'Now,' I said, 'if you are the meanest thief in Minneapolis you are certainly a sinner, and that verse says that God loves sinners.' It broke the man's heart, and he commenced to weep. I took him to my office with me, and we sat down and he told me his story. He said, 'I am just out of confinement. I was released from prison this morning. I had started out this evening with some companions that I knew to commit one of the most daring burglaries that ever was committed in this city, and by tomorrow morning I would either have had a big stake of money or a bullet in my body. But as we were going down the street together we passed the corner where you were holding that open-air meeting. You had a Scotchman speaking. My mother was a Scotchwoman, and when I heard that Scotch tongue it reminded me of my mother. I had a dream about my mother the other night in prison. I dreamed that my mother came to me and begged me to give up my wicked life, and when I heard that Scotchman talk I stepped up to listen. My two pals said, "Come along," and cursed me. I said, "I am going to listen to what this man says." Then they tried to drag me across the street, but I would not go. What that man said touched my heart, and when you gave out the invitation to the meeting I came, and that is why I am here.' I opened my Bible, and I showed that man from the Bible that God loves sinners, how Christ had died for sinners, how he could be saved by simply accepting Christ then and there, and then and there he did accept Christ. We knelt down side by side, and that man offered the most wonderful prayer, but one, I ever heard in all my life.

Is there a thief here tonight? God loves you. Is there a pick-pocket here tonight? God loves you. Is there a lost woman here tonight? God loves you. Is there an infidel here tonight? God loves you. Is there a blasphemer here tonight? God loves you. I will tell you something you can't find in all Birmingham. You can't find in all Birmingham a man or woman that God doesn't love.

GOD'S LOVE IS A HOLY LOVE

The second thing our text teaches us about the love of God is that God's love is a holy love. 'God *so* loved the world, that He gave His only begotten Son.' A great many people cannot understand that. They say, 'I cannot see why it is if God loves me that He doesn't forgive my sins outright without His Son dying in my place. I cannot see the necessity of Christ's death. If God is love, and if God loves me and loves everybody, why doesn't He take us to heaven right away without Christ dying for us.' The text answers the question, 'God *so* loved, *so* loved.' That 'so' brings out the character of God's love. It was of such a character that God could not and would not pardon sin without an atonement. God is a holy God. God's love is a holy love. Now, God's holiness, like everything in God, is real. There is no sham in God. It is real love, real rightousness, and real holiness, and God's holiness, since it is real, must manifest itself in some way. It must either manifest itself in the punishment of the sinner - that is, in our eternal banishment from Him, in your ruin and in mine - or it must manifest itself in some other way. Now, the atoning death of Jesus Christ upon the cross of Calvary was God substituting His atoning action whereby He expressed His hatred of sin for His punitive action whereby He would have expressed the same thing. But some man says, 'That is not just. The doctrine you teach is this - that God, the first Person, took the sin of man, the second person, and laid it upon Jesus Christ, an innocent third Person, and that is not just.' Well, that would not be just, but that is not what the Bible teaches, and that is not what I teach. I don't teach and the Bible doesn't teach, that God, a holy first Person, takes the sins of you and me, guilty second persons, and lays them upon Jesus Christ, an innocent third Person. Jesus Christ was not a third Person. 'God was in Christ reconciling the world unto Himself,' and the atoning death of Jesus Christ on the cross is not God taking my sin off from me and laying it on a third person; it is God the Father taking the penalty of my sin into His own heart, and dying in His Son, in whom He personally dwelt, in place of the rebel. And again, Jesus Christ was not merely the first Person. He was the second Person too. Jesus Christ was the Son of Man, the second Adam, the representative man. No ordinary man could have died for you and me. It would have been of no value. But Jesus Christ was the second Adam, the second head of the race, the second Person, your representative and mine, and when Christ died on the cross of Calvary, I died in Him, and the penalty of my sin was paid. Friends, the philosophy of the Atonement as laid down in the Bible is the most profound and wonderful philosophy the world ever saw or heard. The Christian doctrine is a perfect whole. You take out one doctrine and the others are irrational, but you put them all together and they are a perfect system. For example, if you become a Unitarian and take out the deity of Christ the Atonement becomes irrational. If you take out the humanity of Christ and have Jesus Christ merely Divine the Atonement becomes irrational. But you take all that the Bible says, that God was in Christ, and that in Christ the Word became flesh, real man, God manifest in the flesh, and the Atonement of Christ is the most profoundly and wonderfully philosophical truth the world has ever seen. God's love was a holy love. I thank God that it was. I thank God that His method was such that in perfect righteousness, and perfect justice and perfect holiness, as well as perfect love, on the ground of Christ's atoning death He could pardon and save the vilest of sinners. And, men and women, when you are awakened to a proper sense of your sinfulness, when you see yourself as you really are, and when you see God as He really is, nothing will satisfy your conscience but the doctrine that God, the Holy One, substituted His atoning action, whereby He expressed His hatred of sin, for His punitive action whereby He would have expressed the same thing, and that in the death of Jesus Christ on the cross of Calvary your sin and mine was perfectly settled for ever.

Thank God, the broken law of God has no claim upon me. I broke it, I admit it, but Jesus Christ kept it, and having kept it, He satisfied its punitive claim by dying for those who had not kept it, and on the ground of that atoning death there is pardon tonight for the vilest sinner. A man sits here in the audience tonight. He says, 'There is no forgiveness for me.' Why not? 'Because I have gone down so deep in sin.' Listen men. You have gone deep into sin; you have gone deeper into sin than you realise yourself, but while your sins are as high as the mountains the atonement that covers them is as high as heaven. While your sins are as deep as the ocean the atonement that swallows them up is as deep as eternity, and on the ground of Christ's atoning death there is pardon tonight for the vilest sinner in Bingley Hall, for the vilest sinner on the face of this earth.

THE GREATNESS OF THAT LOVE

The third thing our text teaches us about the love of God is THE GREATNESS OF THAT LOVE. 'God so loved the world, that He gave His only begotten Son, that whosoever believeth in Him should not perish, but have everlasting life.' The greatness of God's love comes out in two ways in the text; first of all, in the greatness of the gift He offers us - eternal life. It does not mean merely a life that is endless in its duration. Thank God, it means that, but it means more; it means a life that is perfect and divine in its quality as well as endless in its duration, and that is what is offered to you tonight. 'God so loved the world, that He gave His only begotten Son, that whosoever believeth in Him should not perish, but have everlasting life.' I do thank God for a life that is perfect in quality and that will never end. Most of us have got to die before long, as far as our physical life is concerned. A large number of this eight or nine thousand people who are now listening to my voice will be in their graves in a few months, more of us in a year, more in five, still more in ten, almost all of us in forty. Eighty years from tonight, probably, there won't be a person on this earth, unless the Lord has come before, who is in this audience tonight. Well, you say, eighty years is a pretty long time. No, it is not. It looks long to you young people. It looks long to look forward to, but when you get to be forty-eight, as I am, and there are thirty-two years of it left, it does not look very long. It looks very short. Eighty years don't look very long, and, friends, when the eighty years are up, what then? Suppose I had a guarantee tonight that I was going to live two hundred years in perfect health, strength, and prosperity. Would that satisfy me? No, it would not; for when the two hundred years are up, what then? Suppose I had a guarantee tonight that I was going to live a thousand years in perfect health and strength, and prosperity. Would that satisfy me? No it would not; for when the thousand years are up, what then? Suppose I had a guarantee tonight that I should live on this earth for ten thousand years in perfect health and strength and prosperity, would that satisfy me? No, it would not; for when the ten thousand years are up, what then? Men, I want something that never ends, and, thank God, in Christ I have got something that never ends. Thousands of years will pass into tens of thousands, tens of thousands will pass into millions, millions will pass into hundreds of millions, hundreds of millions will pass into billions, and the billions will pass into trillions and I will be living on, and on, and on, in ever-growing joy and glory. Eternal life! Eternal life! And who can have it? Anybody. 'Whosoever believeth in Him.'

What does 'whosoever' mean? Somebody asked a little boy once, 'What does whosoever mean?' and the little fellow answered, 'It means you and me and everybody else.' Thank God, it does. It means you and me and everybody else. Somebody once said - I think it was John Bradford - that he was glad that John 3:16 did not read that "God so loved the world, that He gave His only begotten Son that John Bradford might have everlasting life," 'for,' he said, 'if it read that way I would be afraid it meant some other John Bradford. But when I read that 'God so loved the world, that He gave His only begotten Son, that WHOSOEVER believeth in Him,' I know that means me.' Thank God, it did, and it means everybody else in this building tonight. Friends I came into this building tonight with a pocket pretty well filled, with shillings and half-crowns, and half-sovereigns, and sovereigns, and cheques, and so on that have come to me through the mail today. They are all gone. I handed them over to the treasurer. But tonight while I go out with an empty pocket I will go out with a full heart - a heart that is full of everlasting life, and that is worth millions of sovereigns. Every other man and woman in this building can go out the same way.

But the text tells us a second way more wonderful yet in which the greatness of the love of God shows itself, and that is in the sacrifice that God made for us. 'God so loved the world, that He gave His only begotten Son.' Now, as I said the other night, the measure of love is sacrifice. You can tell just how much anybody loves you by the sacrifice that he is willing to make for you. God had shown the measure of His love by the sacrifice He made. What was it? His very best. He 'so loved the world that He gave His only begotten Son,' the dearest that He had. No earthly father ever loved his son as God loved Jesus Christ. I have an only son; how I love him. We have oftentimes wished that God in His kindness had given us three or four sons provided they were all like the one He gave us, just as He has given us four daughters; but I was thinking of it this afternoon, and this thought occurred to me, that perhaps the reason why God had only given us but one son was that I might have a little deeper realisation of how much God loved Jesus Christ. Friends, suppose some day I should see that boy of mine arrested, suppose he went as a missionary to China, and I saw him arrested by the enemies of Christ; and suppose they blindfolded him, and then they spat in his face, and then they punched him in his face, and then plaited a crown of great big cruel thorns and put it on his brow, and then some Chinaman should come along and with a heavy stick knock that crown down upon his brow until the blood poured down his face on either side. How do you suppose I would feel? Then suppose they took him, and stripped his garments from him, and took him to a post, made him lean over until the skin of his back was all drawn tight, and bound him to the post, and a soldier came along with a long stick that had on the end long lashes of leather in which were twisted bits of brass and lead, then that soldier laid the lash upon the boy's back thirty-nine times till it was all torn and bleeding, and my son's back was one mass of bloody wounds. How do you think I would feel? Then suppose they took him and laid a cross down upon the ground and stretched his right hand out on the arm of the cross, put a nail in the hand, lifted the heavy hammer and drove the nail through the hand; then stretched his left arm on the other arm of the cross, put a nail in the palm of that hand, and lifted the heavy hammer and sent the nail through that hand, then put a nail through his feet, and lifted the heavy hammer and drove the nail through his feet, and then took that cross to which he was nailed and plunged it into a hole on a rock, and left him hanging there, the agony getting worse and worse every minute. See him hanging there beneath the burning sun from nine o'clock in the morning till three o'clock in the afternoon, and I standing and looking on as my only boy dies in awful agony on a cross. How do you suppose I would feel? But, men, that is just what God saw. He loved His only begotten Son, as you and I never dreamt of loving our sons. He saw them spit in His face; He saw them blindfold Him; He saw them smite Him with their fists; He saw them take rods and beat Him with rods; He saw them take the crown of awful thorns and press it on His brow, and then smite it down with a heavy rod; He saw them strip the garments from off His back, tie Him to a post, make Him lean over until the skin upon His back was drawn tight; then He saw a brawny Roman soldier take that awful scourge with long leather lashes into which were twisted bits of brass and lead, and lay it on His back thirty-nine times till it was one mass of aching wounds. He saw them take Him and stretch Him on a cross, drive a nail into that hand, drive a nail into His feet, and take that cross and plunge it into a hole on that rock, and leave Him hanging there, aching, all His bones out of joint, tortured in every member of His body! God looked on. Why did He suffer it? Because He loved you and me, and it was the only way that you and I could be saved, and 'God so loved the world, that He gave His only begotten Son, that whosoever believeth in Him should not perish, but have everlasting life.'

Men, how are you going to repay that love tonight? I know how some of you are going to repay it. You are going to repay it with hatred. You hate God. You never said it, but it is true.

A friend of mine was preaching one time in Connecticut. He was stopping with a physician who had a beautiful amiable daughter. She had never made a profession of religion, but she was such a beautiful character that people thought she was a Christian. One night, after the meetings had been going on some time, my friend said to this young lady, 'Are you not going up to the meeting tonight?' She said, 'No Mr. Hammond, I am not.' 'Oh,' he said, 'I think you had better go.' She said, 'I will not go.' 'Why,' he said 'don't you love God?' She said, 'I hate God.' She had never realised it before. I think she would have said she loved God up to that time, but when the demands of God were pressed home by the Holy Spirit she was not willing to obey, and she found out that she hated God.

Some of you have never found it out - that you hate God, but it is true. How some of you used the name of God today. You have used it many times. In prayer? No, in profanity. Why? Because you hate God. Some of you men here tonight, if your wives should take Christ in this meeting and go home, you would make life unendurable. Why? Because you hate God, and you are going to make your wife miserable for accepting His Son. Some of you young people, if some other young person in your shop, or your factory, or your mill should accept Christ tonight, you would laugh at them for it tomorrow. Why? Because you hate God. Some of you people will read every infidel book you can get, you will go to every infidel lecture. You are trying to convince yourself that the Bible is not God's Word, and if anybody would come along and bring up some smart objection to the Bible, you would laugh at it and rejoice in it. Why? Because you hate God, and you want to get rid of God's Book. Some of you men and women here tonight, you just love to hold up your heads and toss them, and say, 'I don't believe in the Divinity of Christ, I don't believe He is the Son of God.' Why? Because you hate God, and if you can rob His divine Son of the honour that belongs to Him, you will do it. You are repaying the wondrous love of God with hate. Some of you are refusing to accept Christ. You have been here night after night during the Mission. People have been down the hall, and when people speak to you you get angry. You say, 'I wish you would not talk to me. Go about your own business. It is none of your business whether I am a Christian or not.' You get angry every time anybody speaks to you. Why? Because you hate God. Some of you so bitterly hate God that you are trying to find fault with the doctrine of the Atonement. You are trying to make yourself believe that Christ did not die on the cross for you. You say, 'I cannot understand the philosophy of it.' If you loved God, you would not stop to ask the philosophy of it. You would simply lift your heart in simple gratitude and praise to God, that He so loved you that He gave His Son to die for you.

THE CONQUERING POWER OF GOD'S LOVE

There is one other thing that our text teaches us about the love of God, and that is, THE CONQUERING POWER OF GOD'S LOVE. 'God so loved the world, that He gave His only begotten Son, that whosoever believeth in Him should not perish, but have everlasting life.' The love of God conquers sin; the love of God conquers death; the love of God conquers wrong, and saves a man from perishing unto everlasting life. And, men and women, the love of God conquers where everything else fails. The first time I ever preached in Chicago - it was several years before I went there to live, I was there at a Convention - after the sermon, among the people who stood up that night to say they wanted to be prayed for, I noticed a young woman who did not come forward when the rest came. I went down to where she was standing and urged her to come forward. She laughed, and said, 'No, I am not going forward,' and sat down again. The next night was not an evangelistic service, but a meeting of the Convention. I was President of the Convention. As I looked over the audience, away down toward the back I saw that young woman in the audience elegantly dressed - the most finely dressed woman in the audience. I called somebody else to the chair, and slipped around to the back part of the building. When the meeting was dismissed, I made my way to where that young lady was sitting. I sat down beside her. I said, 'Won't you take Christ tonight?' 'No,' she said; 'would you like to know the kind of life I am living?' It was not known that she was living that kind of life. She was living it in the best society, honoured and respected. Then she commenced to unfold to me one of the saddest stories of dishonour I ever listened to, without blushing, laughing as if it was a joke; and finally she said, 'Let me tell you how I spent last Easter.' I cannot tell you how it was - how any woman of any sense could have told it to any man I cannot imagine - and when she had told the story she burst out into a laugh, and said, 'That was a funny way to spend Easter, wasn't it?' I was dumbfounded. I simply took my Bible - I had a little Bible with fine print - and opened it at John 3:16, passed it over to her, and said, 'Won't you please read that?' She had to hold it very near her eyes to see the print, and she commenced in a laughing way. 'God so loved' - she was laughing no more - 'the world' - there was nothing like a laugh now - 'that He gave His only begotten Son.' And she burst into tears, and literally the tears flowed down on to the elegant silk robe that she was wearing. Hardened as she was, brazen as she was, shameless as she was, trifling as she was, one glimpse of Jesus on the Cross of Calvary for her had broken her heart. God grant that it may break your's tonight.

I want to tell you one more incident before I sit down. One night I was preaching, and we had an after-meeting. The leading soprano in my choir was not a Christian. I don't believe in having an unconverted choir; we don't allow anybody in our choir in Chicago who is not a converted person to the best of our knowledge. You say, 'You must have a pretty small choir.' We have two hundred, and every one of them as far as we know, is converted. But in that church it was not so, and my leading soprano was not a Christian- a gay, worldly girl, not immoral at all, a very respectable girl, but very worldly and very gay. She stayed to the after-meeting. Her mother rose down in the body of the house and said, 'I wish you would all pray for the conversion of my daughter.' I did not look round at the choir, but I knew perfectly well how that young woman looked, without looking round. I knew her cheeks were burning, I knew her eyes were flashing, and I knew that she was very angry from the crown of her head to the sole of her feet. Just as soon as the meeting was over, I hurried down to the particular door that I knew she would have to pass out by. A she came along I advanced toward her, held out my hand, and said, 'Good evening, Cora.' Her eyes flashed, and her cheeks burned. She did not take my hand. She stamped her foot and said, 'Mr. Torrey, my mother knows better than to do what she has done tonight. She knows it will only make me worse.' I said, 'Cora, sit down.' The angry girl sat down, and I opened my Bible at Isaiah 53:5, and handed it to her. I said, 'Won't you please read it?' And she read, 'He was wounded for our transgressions, He was bruised for our iniquities, the chastisement of our peace was laid upon Him.' She did not get any further; she burst into tears; the love of God revealed in the Cross of Christ had broken her heart. I left the city the next day. While I was away I got a letter saying that this young lady was happily converted, but very ill. I returned to Minneapolis, called at the house, found her rejoicing in Christ, but so ill that the physician held out no hope of her recovery. A few days later, her brother came running up to my house in the morning about ten o'clock. He said, 'Mr. Torrey, come down to the house just as quick as you can. Cora has been unconscious all morning. She has not spoken a word. She hardly seems to be breathing. She is as white as marble, and we think she is dying. She seems to be utterly unconscious.' I hurried down there. And there lay the whitest living person I had ever seen, bleeding to death through her gums and nose. She was perfectly unconscious apparently, and had not said a word all the morning. Her mother stood at the foot of the bed with a breaking heart. 'Oh,' she said. 'Mr. Torrey, pray, pray, please pray!' I knelt down by the bedside and prayed. I didn't suppose the girl had heard a word I said. I was praying to comfort her mother. And just as soon as I had finished my prayer, there came from those white lips, in a clear, strong, full, beautiful voice, the most wonderful prayer I have ever heard in my life. The dying girl said, 'O, Heavenly Father, I want to live if it be Thy will, so that as I have sung in the past for my own glory, I can sing for the glory of Jesus, Who loved me, and gave Himself for me. Father, I want to live, but if Thou dost not see fit to raise me up from this bed, I shall be glad to depart and be with Christ.' And she departed to be with Christ. The love of God had conquered.

Men and women, let the love of God conquer your stubborn, wicked, foolish, sinful, worldly, careless hearts tonight. 'God so loved the world, that He gave His only begotten Son, that whosoever believeth in Him should not perish, but have everlasting life.' Yield to that love tonight. Amen.

DR. WALTER L. WILSON MD

We learn from 'Who's Who in America' (vol. 26) that Dr. Walter L. Wilson graduated from high school in Kansas City, studied medicine in Northwestern University and received his MD from the University of Kansas in 1904. Bob Jones University in South Carolina, also honoured him with a Doctor of Letters degree in 1937.

He helped to found the Kansas City Bible Institute in 1932, and he also carried on a daily Bible Exposition broadcast for many years.

He was the author of a number of books and pamphlets on Christian subjects. Several of them relate his personal work experience, namely *Romance of a Doctor's Visits; Miracles in a Doctor's Life; Strange Experiences of the Doctor;* and *Remarkable New Stories.* His book *The Doctor's Best Love Story* contains seventeen expositions based on John 3:16. In this book Dr. Wilson says: 'This verse may be described as "God's Treasure Chest." In these few words there is presented the sweetest treasure of all, for the greatest need of all, and this treasure is sufficient for all.' The following sermon is taken from this volume.

10

SEVEN PRECIOUS TRUTHS IN JOHN 3: 16

We apply the word 'Precious' to jewels and to babies. It describes that object which is dear to our hearts, either because of relationship, or because of its potential or actual value. Here in John 3:16 are seven 'precious' truths. Surely we should treasure them as a priceless asset to our souls.

A SACRED PERSON

This blessed One is brought before us for the attention of our hearts and the meditation of our minds as we read the Word of 'GOD'. The Lord Jesus immediately takes our attention in this passage to the most wonderful and holy Person in all the universe. We are invited to think of Him, to look at Him, to meditate on Him, to lean on Him, to listen to Him, to consider Him, and to heed His words. What a blessed privilege it is for mortal man to know the eternal God!

God dwells in light unapproachable, as well as in darkness impenetrable. He dwells in the high and holy place, which no human eye has seen and no human hand has reached. He rides upon the wind and walks upon the clouds, where no human foot ever has trod or can tread. God is a holy God. No iniquity can dwell in His presence; no sin can touch His holy throne. His eyes are too pure to behold iniquity. He sits upon a white throne unspotted and untouched by the wickedness of men. Without formality, Christ Jesus introduces us to this serene and sacred Sovereign of the universe.

By the word of His mouth He placed a billion stars in their sockets of blue. By the breath of His mouth He made the myriads of fish in the sea. At His command there sprang into being the endless varieties of beetles and bugs, butterflies and birds, and at His command they are fed, kept, and reproduced. This great and majestic God, mighty in His power and matchless in His beauty, is revealed to us by these wonderful words of our precious Lord in John 3:16.

'That Thou shouldst love a wretch like me,
And be the God Thou art
Is darkness to my intellect,
But sunshine to my heart.'

A STRONG PASSION

Love for lost men is the outstanding characteristic of God, and is revealed to us in the words 'so loved.' Love is said to be the strongest passion in the world. Love will overcome every obstacle and find the object of its love, though it traverse sea and land, mountain and valley, shop and home. The lad who was kidnapped had a father who loved him. Every force of the law, every instrument of the government, every human device that was obtainable, was commandeered for the purpose of finding the son whom the father loved. When a message was received demanding a tremendous ransom, the father immediately made arrangements to fulfil the demand, and did everything possible to obtain the money and deliver it to the abductors in the manner prescribed. Love paid the price to obtain the person that was loved.

Love will pursue its object in every possible way; by train and by auto the chase is made; by ship and by airplane the chase continues. Neither time, nor distance, nor the elements will interfere with this pursuit. Love schemes and plans in order to be with the object of its devotion. Love will risk health and wealth, possessions and positions, and will make any sacrifice, if it can only have that one on whom it has set its desires.

Here in John 3:16 is revealed the supreme love of all loves. It is the strongest of all loves, because it has accomplished the greatest ends. This love was willing to give the most marvellous of all gifts. This love reached to the highest throne to give a love gift to the worst of men, the lowest of sinners. This love loves all between the highest and the lowest; none are omitted, all are included. This love is for YOU.

A SINFUL PEOPLE

These are the objects of this strong passion in the sacred heart of the eternal God. Sin has wrecked the lives of men. Sin has penetrated the palace of the king, the home of the peasant, and the houses of those in poverty. Tears attest its presence, sighs acclaim its cruelty, graves announce its ferocity. The presence of the police proves the presence of sin. Courts prosecute it; jailors seek to correct it; doctors treat it; the world's wealth pays for it.

Sin penetrates and permeates all society. Sin infects and afflicts. Sin fills the battlefields with the dead and asylums with the demented. Sin creates orphans and widows and fills graveyards. Sin wounds but never heals; sin brings sorrow without a solace. Sin cries constantly for more, it has an insatiable greed, it is never satisfied. Sin cares not for the damage it causes and recognises no master nor law. Sin strikes at God's throne, and is an enemy of righteousness and of the rights of others. Sin has its devotees everywhere - alert, persistent, cunning, and zealous. Its advertisements are everywhere - attractive, alluring, colourful, and exciting.

Sin calls for the skill of the artist, the painter, the carpenter, the inventor, the musician, the printer, and the manufacturer. Sin lays a heavy toll on its participants to pay the bill, and then cruelly demands payment. The shores of time are strewn with the wreckage of sin, and the debris of many walls built by men to stop its progress and hinder its course is seen on every hand. Sin is the most prized of all possessions. Kings will lose a crown and forfeit a kingdom for it. Wise men will prostitute their wisdom to enjoy it. Wealthy men will fling away their riches to obtain it. Those who seek for it will die for it, will break up the finest home for it, will sever the dearest ties for it, will cast away their health and honour to obtain it. Men will forfeit all that is good and true and noble and pure, for a brief hour upon its bosom. Men will ignite an unquenchable fire, and face the dark portals of an endless hell, for a sip from the cup of sin. Oh, the awfulness of sin!

Great foundations have been established to study its causes and to effect a cure. The greatest minds are conscripted to invent ways and means of successfully combating it. The skill of the physician, the care of the nurse, and the services of the druggist are called upon to extinguish the flames of sin, and to repair the damage which it has wrought. Businessmen are against it; society is against it; teachers are against it; parents are against it; but among all these we find no cure. God is against sin; Christ is against sin; the Holy Spirit is against sin; the Bible is against sin; the Church is against sin.

In the beautiful verse we are considering is disclosed God's remedy for a SINFUL PEOPLE. Only the love of God can conquer sin; only the blood of Christ can wash it away; only the Holy Spirit can prevent it; only the Word of God can supplant it.

God gave Christ to save you from its penalty, and now Christ will give you His life to save you from its power. The Holy Spirit gives you His Word to save you from its deceptions. Is sin driving you, or are you driving it? Are you saved from it, or condemned by it? Are you for it, or against it? Do you encourage it, or deny it? Do you feed it, or fight it? Do you hate it, or love it? God's remedy for sin is Calvary. God's reward for sin is the lake of fire. A sinful people may become a saved people, because of the strong passion of this sacred God.

A STRIKING PROOF

The evidence of God's rich provision for a sinful people is given to us in the words of Christ: 'He gave His only begotten Son.' How often the question is asked, 'How do I know that you love me?' Love must be shown; love must be proved; love must be experienced. God could have told us that He loved us and given no other evidence than the great gifts of creation. God could have said that He loved us and left us to believe it or to doubt it as we might choose.

God knew the frailty of the human mind and heart. God knew the desire of men to realise and to understand by his senses. Therefore, God has given us an unmistakable, undeniable, and unavoidable proof of the secret love that was in His heart, which He desired to reveal to us openly. Is it proof that you want? Then look at Bethlehem and the manger, or at Calvary and the Cross, or at the crown on Christ's head in the glory. Do you want still further proof? Then go with Him into the wilderness as He spent forty days among the wild beasts and was tempted by Satan, that He might prove to you that He can safely be trusted as the sinless Saviour of men.

You may still have further proof of His love if you will go with Him to Gethsemane, and see Him in agony and anguish of spirit, lying prone upon the ground, suffering because He was about to take *your* place. Do you know of anything more that He could have done which would convince you of His great love for you? What further proof would you like to have? What additional evidence do you demand? What other facts do you ask, in order that your heart may be fully convinced that God loves you, and has provided for you in Jesus Christ a perfect Lord, a sufficient Saviour, and a wonderful salvation?

A SIMPLE PLAN

The plan as portrayed in John 3:16 is found in those two words, 'whosoever believeth.' God could have put the way of salvation upon a very expensive basis. Salvation is worth it. Is heaven not a valuable present? A priceless goal? Is it not worth more than we are able to comprehend to escape the wrath to come and receive the love of God? Is it not priceless beyond compare to receive forgiveness of sins here and now, and thus avoid the great white throne judgement?

When such a tremendous salvation, so valuable, so precious, so wonderful, is to be obtained, it would have been quite in keeping if God had priced it at a very high valuation and demanded some great thing from men, in order that they might obtain of it. It is because of God's love that He has made the plan simple. If salvation should only be offered to those who obtain certain scholastic degrees, then untold multitudes would never have an opportunity to be saved. Many in enlightened lands do not have the mental capacity to earn a degree, but God's salvation is for them. Millions live in the darkness of heathendom where colleges are not available, and where educational institutions of all kinds are unthought of, but God's salvation is for them. Many who have the mental ability do not have the financial resources whereby they may go to college and obtain a degree, but God offers His salvation to them. There are those who are afflicted with crippled bodies or with disease and who are, therefore, unable to attend any kind of institution of learning, but they, too, are included in God's simple plan of salvation.

If salvation were obtained by lifting up the hand of five times towards heaven, then those who are paralysed would be shut out. If salvation should be offered to those who will walk in a straight line for fifteen feet, then all the cripples and the bedridden would be hopeless, for they could not fulfil the condition. If salvation should be on sale for a nickel or a dime, then millions could not have it, for multitudes have no money and never see any money. God has made the plan so simple that He may include all and exclude none, and that this great gift of eternal life may be within the reach of every living person, and may not be out of reach of a single soul.

How *we should* thank God for this simple plan! God grant that we may be simple enough ourselves to take with simplicity and by simple faith this simple plan which brings such blessed and eternal results. 'He that hath the Son hath life' (1 John 5:12).

A SURE PLEDGE

This pledge is given to every believer in Jesus Christ - to everyone who takes God at His word. This token of truth, this proof of fact is extended to us in these beautiful words, 'should not perish.' How do we know that the believer will not perish? Because we have His word for it. What greater pledge could we have than the word of One who cannot lie? What greater assurance could we have than the word of the eternal God who has never failed? His Word is immutable and imperishable. There is not a shadow of doubt or of darkness in His Word. 'God is not a man, that He should lie; ... hath He said, and shall He not do it? or hath He spoken, and shall He not make it good?'

The Word of God standeth sure! No one can alter it and nothing can change it. If He said 'should not perish' to one who is a believer in Jesus Christ, then that believer will never perish. There is no doubt about it, nor is there any question. God will keep His Word! God will perform His promise! God will maintain the truth of the words which He has spoken!

When Napoleon said to the brave soldier who saved his life, 'Thank you, Captain,' the private soldier became a captain immediately. The word of the Emperor was sufficient. The word of the supreme commander was also recognised by the other officers, and the private soldier was immediately received as one of the captains of the regiment.

When Wellington wrote 'I will pay' beneath the list of the soldier's debts, as the soldier was sleeping, that burdened soldier knew that his commanding officer would lift the load from his heart and would pay his obligations. The general's word brought peace to the troubled private.

The burdened nobleman believed the word of Christ and went his way in peace, believing that his son was cured. He had only the word of his Lord, nothing else; nothing else was needed. This story is told in John 4:46-53. The word of our God is a sufficient pledge to every trusting heart. 'The word of the Lord endureth for ever' (1 Peter 1:25).

149

A STERLING POSSESSION

The gift of life is the blessed present portion of every true believer in the Son of God. The possession of eternal life is the greatest possession possible to a human being. Other possessions may be taken from us by thieves and robbers, but no one can take Christ from the believing heart. Other possessions fade and fail, rust out, or wear out, but this blessed possession grows richer and rarer, brighter and more beautiful as the years go by.

Some possessions become a burden as taxes increase, but this blessed possession lifts the load from heavy laden hearts and makes the burden lighter. This possession fits for eternity and prepares the Christian for that long experience in the heavenly kingdom. Other possessions cease their usefulness at the grave, but this possession is of value in the sunset days, when the shadows are falling, as well as in the early years of life. This possession enriches the soul, even when the riches of earth abound, and it also fills the heart with rest, the mind with peace, and the soul with joy, even when riches make themselves wings and flee away.

This priceless portion satisfies the craving of the heart when the feet fail to carry the body, and the eyes fail to see the light; when the ears can no longer hear, and the tongue cannot discern between sweet and sour; even then He still remains a precious portion for the heart of the trusting saint. To have Christ is to have life. Christ is our life. The life of God is in the Son of God. 'He that *hath* the Son *hath* life.' God gave Christ to you, so that in having Him you would have this sterling possession of eternal life. This possession links you with God. This possession equips you to enjoy God. This possession makes it possible for you to live with God. This possession will give you an understanding heart that can understand God. God grant that you may make Christ Jesus your own, so that with Him you may have everlasting life forever.

AMBASSADOR

Other titles available by/on the Preachers of the sermons contained in this book, available from Ambassador Publications include:-

A Pathway of Roses/Boreham	(£4.50)
Comfort and Assurance/Spurgeon	(£6.99)
Evangelism/Spurgeon	(£6.99)
George Muller/Pierson	(£8.99)
God's Treasury/Spurgeon	(£5.99)
The Greatest Fight in the World/Spurgeon	(£4.99)
The Holy Spirit/Torrey	(£4.99)
John Poughman's Talk/Spurgeon	(£4.99)
The Lord's Return/Torrey	(£4.99)
Love So Amazing/Moyer	(£2.75)
Miracles/Spurgeon	(£6.99)
Parables/Spurgeon	(£6.99)
Pastor in Prayer/Spurgeon	(£4.99)
Prayer/Spurgeon	(£6.99)
Psalms/Spurgeon	(£6.99)
Revival/Spurgeon	(£6.99)
Shall we know one another in Heaven?/Ryle	(£3.99)
Wind and Fire/Spurgeon	(£4.50)
The C. H. Spurgeon Collection/Spurgeon	(£42.99)

- A set of seven books including: Comfort & Assurance, Evangelism, Miracles, Parables, Prayer, Psalms and Revival.

All titles are available from your Local Christian Bookshop or direct from Ambassador Productions (please send cheque with order/free postage!)